Astrology for Wimps

Astrology for Wimps

Sasha Fenton

Sterling Publishing Co., Inc
New York

Created by Lynn Bryan, The BookMaker, London
Design by Mary Staples
Photography by James Duncan
Edited by Maggie McCormick
Planets created by Badcock and Fruitful

**Library of Congress Cataloging-in-Publication
Data Available**

10 9 8 7 6 5 4 3 2 1

Published by Sterling Publishing Co., Inc.
387 Park Avenue South, New York, NY 10016
© 2003 by Sasha Fenton

Printed in China
Sterling ISBN 1-4027-0384-8

Distributed in Canada by
Sterling Publishing
c/o Canadian Manda Group,
One Atlantic Avenue, Suite 105,
Toronto, Ontario, Canada M6K 3EZ

Distributed in Great Britain by Chrysalis Books
64 Brewery Road, London N7 9NT, England

Distributed in Australia by Capricorn Link
(Australia) Pty. Ltd.
P.O. Box 704, Windsor, NSW 2756, Australia

To Jonathon Dee, astrologer extraordinaire

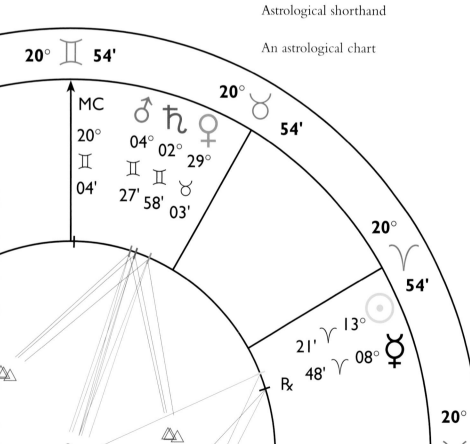

Contents

Astrology for wimps!

Astrology cannot cause physical discomfort or danger, and it is hardly likely to encourage evil spirits to climb out of the closet and disturb your nights or frighten your children. There is a wrong perception that astrology is difficult, that it involves poring over complicated mathematical tables and spending time on difficult numerical calculations. It is true that a

Hold that thought! . . .

What is there to be frightened of?

professional astrologer needs to know a huge amount, but an ordinary person like you doesn't need to become a professor. If wimps are **people who want to understand** *themselves*, *their friends*, and their *loved ones,* and *to peer into the mists of the future*, *a basic knowledge of astrology is just perfect for them.*

As an A-grade wimp, I took up astrology in my youth because I needed to understand how other people operated, and why they sometimes did things I considered incomprehensible. I soon found myself unlocking the secrets behind the character of the people in my circle, and understanding the reasons for their behavior.

All my single women friends are total wimps. The first thing they do when a new man swans into their lives is to ask me to run a check on him. When they know the poor man's faults and failings, they can decide to jump into a relationship with him, or abort their mission. If they decide to go ahead, at least they know what they are buying into. Consider this: what man would wish to tie himself up to a woman who spends money as though it was going out of fashion? What woman would want to get into a relationship with a man who was likely to fool around with half the women in the county? Knowledge is power—and wimps need as much as they can get their hands on!

All astrologers are wimps, because none of us is prepared to go through life blinded to the reality of the personalities we draw around us. With no more than a date of birth to go on, we can see where people are coming from, and how they are likely to impact upon our lives. When we have a date, time, and place of birth, we pick someone apart in the same way Sigmund Freud and his pals could do—and we don't need to grapple with long words while doing it.

No astrologer can predict the future with absolute clarity, but we can spot upcoming trends and take advantage of them. When the trends look crummy, we can use foreknowledge to sidestep the worst of them. Even if we can't avoid problems, we can work out how long they will go on—which makes them easier to bear. An astrology chart is like a road map of the future, and what self-respecting wimp would embark on a tricky journey without one?

In astrology there are really only 12 factors to learn, and chances are you know some of them already. The 12 factors are the 12 signs of the zodiac from Aries through to Pisces. You already know something about your own nature and that of your partner, children, parents, and best friends. So, unless there is something really unusual on their horoscopes that makes them extremely atypical for their signs, you can put your knowledge of this group to others who share their sun signs. If you know from personal experience how restless your Sagittarian partner can be or how practical your Taurean son is (most of the time), you can apply this knowledge to others who share those sun signs. All you need to do is to learn the signs that you are less familiar with. Most astrology is a matter of fitting these 12 factors together in a variety of patterns.

There are a few more factors for the braver wimp to grapple with, and they are explained in this book. Take a small percentage of these topics on board and you will be—an astrologer!

You will dazzle your friends with your erudition. Yes, studying astrology does mean giving your brain an outing, but only to the extent of gaining an insight into such vital matters as these:

Why does your pretty female friend pile on enough makeup to plaster a wall?
(She's a Taurus with Venus in Leo.)

Why does your boss keep his small change in a tiny wallet?
(He's a Capricorn with Jupiter in Scorpio.)

Why is your male friend paying a fortune to have a hair transplant on his bald spot?
(He's a Leo with Mercury in Virgo.)

Why does your mother think that you don't eat properly?
(No jokes, please—the woman's a Cancerian.)

Why are you reading this book?
Because you want to know why—that's why.

Good luck!

Sasha Fenton

The

Basics

This chapter sets out to demystify the jargon in astrology, and then explains some of the steps involved in understanding how astrology works and how it can assist you in your life.

What is astrology?

The word "astrology" means a study of the stars. "Astronomy" is a study of the heavenly bodies for scientific

purposes, while astrology looks at the way the movement of the planets and constellations in the sky affects all of us.

The position of certain planets, star groups, and other celestial features at the time of birth can explain character with amazing accuracy. Astrology can also be used to predict trends and events. Both astrology and astronomy grew out of the early human need to fix a reliable calendar for farming, harvesting, and so on. Astrology was taught in many European universities until the 1600s when a more rational approach to the world was adopted by thinkers. When scientific discoveries of the industrial revolution changed the world, the two systems diverged. Astrology was consigned to the medieval junkyard of signs, omens, witchcraft, and magic.

Now, however, we are accustomed to seeing our horoscopes in newspapers and magazines, which put astrology in the form of a list. Astrologers, though, do it in a circle! If you arrange the familiar newspaper list in a circular shape, you will be thinking like an astrologer, rather than a wimp!

Knowing ourselves and understanding others can help us to get along in life. Knowing trends and events that are likely to affect us as the days, weeks, and months roll by can help us avoid some of life's slings and arrows.

In astrology, there are three factors to get to grips with and they are:

1. **The 12 signs of the zodiac**

2. **The 12 astrological houses**

3. **The 10 planets**

Astrology is based on the relationships between the planets, the sun, the moon, the 12 zodiac signs, and the 12 areas of a person's life, which are known as houses.

On the face of it, this means 36 factors to learn. Each sign, however, is similar to each house, and each planet is associated with a sign and so it shares the same character. Therefore, there are only 12 factors.

Readers of horoscopes are used to seeing each star sign printed in a list, yet astrologers work everything out in a circle.

12 SIGNS OF THE ZODIAC

What's a zodiac? It is a beltway of stars that the sun appears to pass through during the course of each year. There are 12 groups of stars in the zodiac, each of which is a familiar sign: Aries, Taurus, and so on.

The signs of the zodiac are always written in the same order, starting with Aries. In ancient times, the start of Spring (which coincided with the start of Aries) represented the start of the year.

They're often also called sun signs because a person born under a specific sign was born when the sun seemed to be passing through that section of the zodiac. You will also have heard them called star signs.

CATEGORIZATION

Each of the 12 zodiac signs falls into three categories: gender, element, and quality.

GENDER

Firstly, the signs are alternately divided into masculine and feminine (yang and yin) signs.

Masculine (yang)

Aries	21 March–19 April
Gemini	21 May–20 June
Leo	23 July–22 August
Libra	23 September–23 October
Sagittarius	22 November–21 December
Aquarius	20 January–18 February

Feminine (yin)

Taurus	20 April–20 May
Cancer	21 June–22 July
Virgo	23 August–22 September
Scorpio	24 October–21 November
Capricorn	22 December–19 January
Pisces	19 February–20 March

ELEMENTS

Secondly, each of the sun signs belongs to one of four elements. Each element has a nature of its own.

Element	Sign
FIRE	Aries, Leo, Sagittarius
EARTH	Taurus, Virgo, Capricorn
AIR	Gemini, Libra, Aquarius
WATER	Cancer, Scorpio, Pisces

Fire signs are quick thinking, fast acting, enthusiastic, and in the forefront of everything that is happening. They are quick to anger, and/or to fall in love.
Earth signs are thorough, reliable, practical, but unadventurous. They fall in love slowly, but once committed, they stick.
Air signs grasp ideas quickly and love to talk them over with others, but move on when new ideas captivate them. They can't stand a boring partner.
Water signs are emotional, imaginative, sensitive, moody and romantic. Impractical and illogical when their feelings rule, they fall deeply in love.

QUALITIES

The qualities represent seasons. They also represent the cardinal points of north, south, east, and west.

Quality	Sign
CARDINAL	Aries, Cancer, Libra, Capricorn
FIXED	Taurus, Leo, Scorpio, Aquarius
MUTABLE	Gemini, Virgo, Sagittarius, Pisces

Cardinal signs mark the start of each season, so these people can work out what is best for themselves. They find it difficult to compromise for the sake of peace.
Fixed signs mark midseason. These people maintain the status quo. They see things through to the end and they don't relish change. They can also be obstinate and determined.
Mutable signs mark the end of each season. These people can adapt to new circumstances. They are often interested in ideas, travel, and spirituality more than advancing in a career.

Is there an Aries in the house?

The houses represent a particular area of life, and it is in each house that the action of the planets is revealed.

SIGN	HOUSE	PLANET
Aries	First house	Mars
Taurus	Second house	Venus
Gemini	Third house	Mercury
Cancer	Fourth house	Moon
Leo	Fifth house	Sun
Virgo	Sixth house	Mercury
Libra	Seventh house	Venus
Scorpio	Eighth house	Pluto
Sagittarius	Ninth house	Jupiter
Capricorn	Tenth house	Saturn
Aquarius	Eleventh house	Uranus
Pisces	Twelfth house	Neptune

QUICK CLUES TO THE HOUSES

Each planet will try to achieve the aim of the house it occupies—but it will do so in its own way. For example, the third house is mainly about interaction and communication. If Mars is here, the person might be an orator, a sportsman, or a salesman. Saturn in the third house belongs to someone who works hard on detailed matters away from the public gaze, and is modest about their achievements.

HOUSE	KEY IDEAS
First	Childhood experiences, the person themselves
Second	Anything valued, possessions, personal wealth
Third	Communication, siblings, local travel
Fourth	Mother, family, home, property
Fifth	Children, creativity, enterprise
Sixth	Health, work
Seventh	Open relationships.
Eighth	Effect of partnerships, shared resources
Ninth	Exploring boundaries of education, law, travel, spirituality
Tenth	Status, ambitions, goals, road to worldly success
Eleventh	Friends, group activities, hopes and wishes
Twelfth	Places of seclusion, artistry, mysticism

PLANETS

The planets are the representatives of different parts of a person's nature, including emotional makeup, mental state, their soul, and their character. The planets are spread around the ecliptic (see page 18) that surrounds the earth, and their placement at the time of your birth in each sign and house is crucial to your personality and makes you unique. See page 50 onward for indepth detail on each of the planets.

SIMILARITIES TO WATCH OUT FOR

By now you will see the link between each sign, house, and planet. You will see the similarity of the character of each sign, house, and planet, such as Aries/first house/Mars. They all share assertive, forthright, honest, and energetic characteristics. Pisces/12th house/Neptune all share a mystical, self-sacrificing nature. By recognizing the relationship between the signs/houses/planets, you will be able to more easily interpret a person's chart.

Once you have established the signs that the individual planets fall into, check to see if there is an emphasis on masculine or feminine signs. Add up how many planets are in each element to see which is emphasized, or if one is deficient in planets. Add the ascendant and the midheaven to this list, too. Check out the qualities to see if one or two qualities are emphasized, if one has a low count, or if there are no qualities at all.

When you have done this, you will have an idea whether the gender balance shows extroversion or introversion, and whether the person is fiery, earthy, airy, or watery. You will also see whether the weighting of the qualities shows the subject to be forward-looking, stick-in-the mud, or happiest just drifting along.

I will explain more about interpretation later in the book.

Our Gemini is looking through a kaleidoscope at the group of stars that makes up her zodiac sign.

A map of the sky

The sun, moon, and all the planets in the solar system lie close to what's known as the ecliptic, so they seem to pass through the various zodiac signs as they make their orbits.

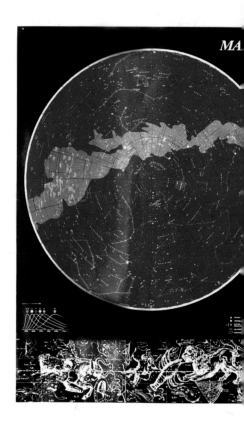

THE ZODIAC BELT

The reason an astrology chart is circular is because it mimics the ecliptic circling the Earth.

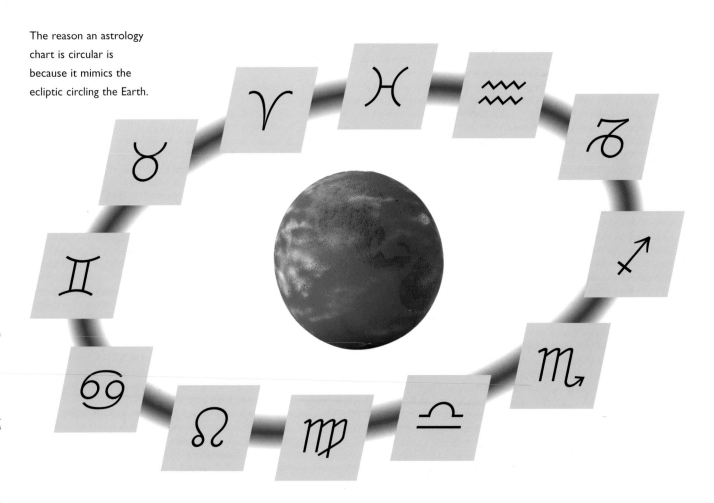

There are a variety of accessories that make studying astrology easier and more entertaining. Here our Gemini is pointing out the group of stars that make up her sun sign.

Since the development of telescopes and the subsequent understanding of the solar system, we know that the moon is the only "planet" that actually orbits the earth. However, from our earthly view of the heavens, it appears that everything revolves around us.

The apparent orbit of the sun is regular and easy to plot because a month is about the amount of time it takes for the sun to travel into a new sign in the zodiac. And, the sun moves through certain constellations (groups of stars each forming a distinctive pattern) at specific times of the year.

We know that the earth orbits the sun, but it looks from our perspective as though the sun follows a path around the earth. This path or trajectory is called the ecliptic. The constellations of stars that lie along the ecliptic must have looked like animals, people, and symbols to ancient people, so they gave them the familiar names (Aries the Ram and Taurus the Bull, and so on) that we use today.

An astrology chart is circular because it mimics the ecliptic circling the earth. While the circle looks remarkably like a clock, the system starts on the left, in the 9 o'clock position, and it runs in a counterclockwise direction.

A birth chart is a map of the sky at the moment of birth. The only time two people can have the same chart is if they are twins—and even then there is always a slight time difference between the first-born and the second. Certain fast-moving features, such as the speedy moon, might have moved a little, even from one sign to the next, and this can make a difference, but the chart is basically the same.

When we start to look at the astrological houses, the position is very different. The starting point for the 12 astrological houses is the rising sign, the sign of the zodiac that was rising over the horizon at the time of a person's birth. Just as the dawn breaks in one location after the other around the earth during the course of a day, so the rising sign also moves right around the earth during the course of a day, through all 12 signs of the zodiac, which means that several people born on the same day will have different rising signs.

Astrological shorthand

Before we go farther, take a look at this glossary of the terms we

have used so far, as well as those you will soon be meeting.

ASCENDANT
The exact degree of the rising sign.

ASPECT
The angle between two or more planets or any other feature on a chart that is formed by the distance these items are from each other around the ecliptic.

BIRTH CHART
The chart for a person, enterprise, business, or political regime at the date, time, and place of birth. It is a unique map of who the person is, and their potential. It shows the positions of the planets in the signs and houses.

CONJUCTION
An aspect (usually good) between two planets that are close to each other.

CUSP
Cusps are the dividing line between the sign and house, and also the start of each house.

DESCENDANT
This is the cusp of your seventh house, representing what you look for in relationships.

ECLIPTIC
The apparent path or trajectory of the sun around the earth during a year.

ELEMENTS
A division of the sun/zodiac signs into fire, earth, air, and water. There are three signs in each element.

HOROSCOPE
Literally, a map of the hour, but it also means the celestial picture at any point in time.

HOUSES
The twelve divisions of the chart, which start from the rising sign.

MIDHEAVEN
In astrology this is at the top of the chart, usually in the ninth or tenth house.

THE PLANETS AND THEIR GLYPHS

GLYPHS
Astrologers use a kind of shorthand called glyphs (from the same root as the word hieroglyphics). They are great time-savers. You'll see these in every astrology book you read. Get familiar with them!

PLUTO

SUN

MOON

MERCURY

VENUS

MARS

JUPITER

SATURN

URANUS

NEPTUNE

MOON SIGN

The sign of the zodiac where the moon was when someone (or something) was born.

NODES

The north node of the moon is the point where the moon crosses the ecliptic in a northward direction on its journey around the earth. The south node is on the opposite side of the horoscope chart.

ORBS

The orb is the number of degrees allowed for any aspect. The conjunction and opposition can have an 8-degree orb, the other aspects all have a 6-degree orb.

PLANETS

The sun, moon, Mercury, Venus, Mars, Jupiter, Saturn, Uranus, Neptune, and Pluto.

OPPOSITION

An aspect (often tense) between two planets that are 180 degrees apart.

QUALITIES

A division of the signs into cardinal, fixed, and mutable. There are four signs in each quality.

RISING SIGN

The sign that rises over the horizon at daybreak at a specific place on the earth.

SEXTILE

An aspect (usually good) between two planets that are around 60 degrees apart.

SUN SIGN

The sign of the zodiac where the sun was when someone (or something) was born.

SQUARE

The aspect (often very tense) between two planets that are 90 degrees apart.

TRINE

The aspect (usually good) between two planets that are about 120 degrees apart.

ZODIAC

The name of the group of stars along the ecliptic path that the sun appears to travel along.

THE STARS AND THEIR GLYPHS

ARIES

LEO

SAGITTARIUS

TAURUS

VIRGO

CAPRICORN

GEMINI

LIBRA

AQUARIUS

CANCER

SCORPIO

PISCES

An astrological chart

Exactly what is an astrological chart? It is circular, like the pie

charts you see in business reports. It is also called a birth chart, or

natal chart, depending upon the astrologer you are dealing with

and where you live.

If you have had your chart done by a professional astrologer, you will be familiar with the circle. This chart holds the key to your life. It is a snapshot of the heavens the moment you were born—the location, the date, and the time you popped out of the womb.

The symbols marked on the chart represent the locations of the planets on that map of the heavens. Each of the 12 sections is known as the house; the symbols (the glyphs) represent the sun/zodiac signs and the planets. (You saw a chart of these on the previous pages.) Practice drawing each of the glyphs until you can match individual symbols with the corresponding sign or planet.

Each sign of the zodiac contains 30 degrees, and the 12 signs make up the 360 degrees of the circle. Every degree contains 60 minutes and, while it isn't vital for a beginner to deal with the minutes of a degree, it is worth knowing what they are and how they are marked on a chart.

Each sign starts at 0 degrees and 0 minutes and ends up at 29 degrees and 59 minutes before its sign changes to the next one. The degrees and minutes

that mark the location of the sun, moon, or any planet are usually expressed this way: "Sun 23° 27' Taurus." So, this person was born when the sun had reached 23 degrees and 27 minutes into the sign of Taurus. Unless an astrologer is doing something especially finicky, he or she will usually only bother with the whole degree, in this case, "Sun 23° Taurus." This location provides enough data on a person.

The upper half of the chart shows where there was daylight and the lower half shows nighttime.

Although we cannot see planets and stars in daylight they are still there. The planets and the constellations of the zodiac above the line would have been in daylight at the time of birth, and those below the line would have been around the other side of the earth, on the dark side of the sky.

Just as the sun rises at dawn, the planets and group of stars that make up a sign of the zodiac also rise. Thus any sign or planet that is somewhere around the arrow on the eastern side of the chart will be rising, and it will give special significance to the chart.

Here is a basic birth
chart showing the main
planets and signs you
will become familiar
with throughout this
book.

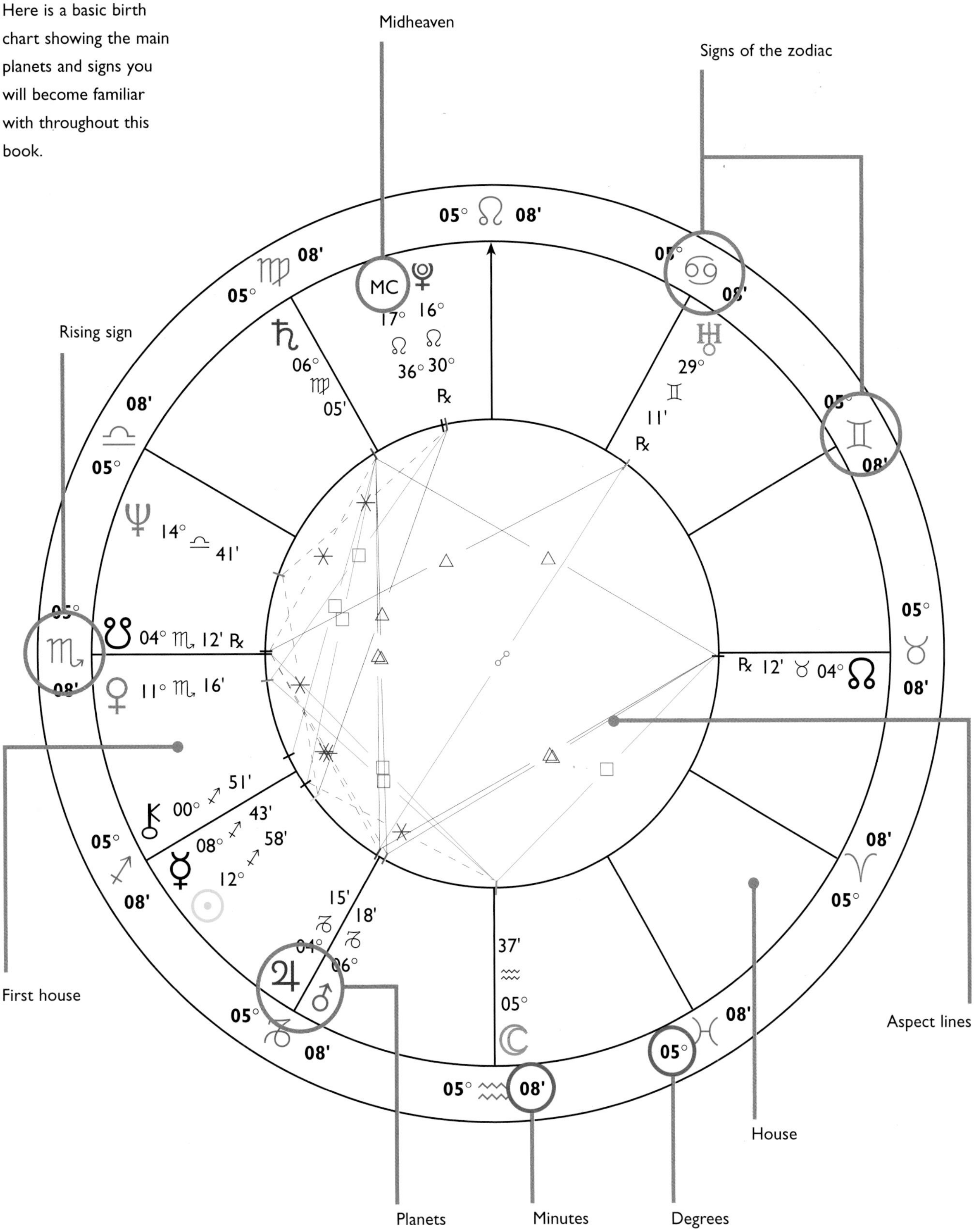

Midheaven

Signs of the zodiac

Rising sign

05° ♌ 08'

08' ♍ 05°

♇ 17° 16°
♆ 36° 30°
Rx

05° ☊ 08'

♄ 06° ♍ 05'

♅ 29° ♊ 11' Rx

08' ♎ 05°

05° ♊ 08'

♆ 14° ♎ 41'

05° 08' ♏

☊ 04° ♏ 12' Rx

♀ 11° ♏ 16'

Rx 12' ♉ 04° ♌

05° 08' ♉

First house

⚷ 00° ♐ 51'
☿ 08° ♐ 43' 58'
12° ♐

05° ♐ 08'

☉

♃ 15° 18'
♂ 04° ♑ 06°

37' ♒ 05°

☽

05° ♑ 08'

08' ♈ 05°

08' ♓ 05°

05° ♓ 08'

05° ♒ 08'

House

Aspect lines

Planets

Minutes

Degrees

Sun

Sun signs have several names: star signs, birth signs, zodiac signs or simply signs, as in, "my sign is Aries." Most of us know our horoscopes by the sun sign. At the start of each sign you'll see the ruling planet, which element the sign is associated with, its quality, the symbol, and the gender.

Astrologers call these the sun signs because from our perspective on earth, the sun appears to travel through each of the signs on fairly regular dates during the year. This is the only aspect of astrology that can be regularly dated and plotted by nonastrologers, which is why it is so popular.

signs

Aries   21 March to 19 April

Symbol: THE RAM

Ruling planet: MARS

Gender: MASCULINE

Element: FIRE

Quality: CARDINAL

Yours is a masculine fire sign, which means you can move quickly when you want. This sign is associated with the self, which is why many Arians are self-centered and unable to sacrifice their needs for those of others. Indeed, they can't even see that others have needs half the time! This doesn't mean that Arians are bad people, just that it is their job in life to ignore what is around them and get things off the ground.

Many of you are courageous, ambitious, and keen to take risks to attain your goals. Some of you can be so dynamic that you unnerve others. Many of you prefer a quiet life, which means you stay in the same job or relationship for many years, due to love, loyalty, or fear of change.

You love your home, and you will try to hang onto your property at all costs, even in tough times. You like to choose the way your home is arranged and decorated, and can argue with a partner about

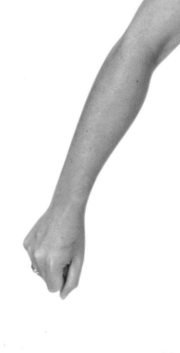

how this should be done, although you probably do the work yourself.

You value loyalty, so you need a partner who is faithful and true to you. You need a lover who understands that your self-confidence sometimes evaporates. Unfortunately, some Arians are not exactly faithful themselves.

You will sacrifice a great deal to make sure your children have all they need, and you see education as the key to success. Never being one to complain, you are terrific in old age. You keep on going, and your sense of humor improves with age. You prefer to work for a large organization, in teaching, or in the political arena, where you feel that what you do is vital.

For such an energetic, courageous person, you don't have a loud voice, and your manner may not reflect the speed at which you think or the speed at which you can act when necessary.

An Arian will take the planet Mars in its stride, kicking it into goal when necessary. There's no messing with this girl.

Taurus   20 April to 20 May

Symbol: THE BULL

Ruling planet: VENUS

Gender: FEMININE

Element: EARTH

Quality: FIXED

Yours is a feminine earth sign, which makes you thorough, sensible, and capable. You can achieve a good deal, as long as you are allowed to do things at your own pace. Astrology books suggest you are dull, dogged, determined, ambitious, and money-minded, but your conversation and sociability make you a welcome addition to any party, while your interests are wide-ranging and your knowledge of your specialized subjects is deep.

You fear poverty and always look for a steady job that gives you a regular income. While some of you are ambitious, many are satisfied to have a safe and

Taurean senses are powerful. Here, her strong artistic sense has come to the fore.

comfortable position in the middle lane. Family life is dear to you, and you are far from tightfisted when it comes to the needs of your loved ones. You can also spend very freely on travel or hobbies.

Many of you can get a bee in your bonnet about something, which means you work hard for whatever cause you decide to take up.

All Taureans have a keen sense of beauty, while many of you have artistic or musical talents. The fields of fashion, decor, makeup, and hair styling appeal to you, which also accounts for the fact that so many of you are found in the supporting casts of show business, where you can cash in on your talent for improving others. Your sensuality and kind heart mean you make a good job of marriage and family life. Your chief fault is obstinacy, and you would be the first to agree that you can dig your heels in, even when it isn't really necessary. Try to see things from other points of view if you are to make sure your friendships and relationships remain peaceful.

Gemini 21 Might to 20 June

Symbol: THE TWINS

Ruling planet: MERCURY

Gender: MASCULINE

Element: AIR

Quality: MUTABLE

Yours is a feminine air sign, so you think and analyze a good deal. You also like to talk on the telephone. You are a true communicator, so you often choose careers that put you in touch with a variety of people, where you can use your charm and sense of humor to make the wheels go around. You need variety in your day-to-day life, but you can also handle detailed figure work, which is why many of you work as accountants. You can show great determination when there is something you are eager to achieve and you can study deeply when something interests you. Many of you are worriers and the things you worry about are probably insignificant, but you can turn yourself into a bag of nerves over something that other people wouldn't think twice about.

During your childhood, you might have been deprived of the security, love, or attention you needed, or you might have had to do without material goods that other children around you had. However, you manage to find love and to make up any material shortages later in life, and many of you would stay with a difficult partner as long as he or she makes good money. You have great homemaking skills, and your home is a warm and comfortable place friends and relatives love to visit.

Your chief indulgences are alcohol and spending money on clothes. You never part with anything once you have bought it, so your wardrobe overflows into closets all around the house.

Your friendly attitude and excellent communication skills mean your social life is great, and you love to get into a car (or aircraft) and travel to visit your family and friends.

Cellphones and
Geminis are made
for each other!

Cancer 21 June to 22 July

Symbol: THE CRAB

Ruling planet: THE MOON

Gender: FEMININE

Element: WATER

Quality: CARDINAL

Yours is a feminine water sign, so you are extremely sensitive to atmospheres, and your emotions are powerful. Being easily hurt, you draw a hard shell around you as emotional protection.

You were probably shy when you were young. You get over this problem to a great extent as you get older, but you still avoid the limelight. Your sign has a reputation for being home-loving, and while you definitely need your own front door and a base to operate from, you also enjoy getting out of the house and traveling. It is possible that you had to grow up quickly, and to take on some family responsibilities when young. When you leave home, you continue to make yourself responsible for others, and you might have more than the average number of children yourself. Cancerians usually stay in touch with all their relatives, so expect plenty of family contact throughout your life.

You find it easy to tap into people's needs and deal with them. Many of you can defuse difficult or even explosive situations, although you can cause some of them when you want to. Many of you work in sales, possibly in retail, or perhaps demonstrating to the public; others work in finance, real estate, or insurance. You are shrewd and bright, and you have plenty of common sense, but your moods and tendency to make decisions from an emotional standpoint can cause problems.

Your main faults are moodiness and your occasional crabby behavior. If you find yourself behaving badly for no discernible reason, look at a calendar to see where the moon is at in its cycle, because you are often bad-tempered or off-color when the moon is full.

Another thing that upsets your equilibrium is a lot of noise and chaos, especially in your own home.

Potentially explosive
situations let a
Cancerian's nerves
get the better of her.

Leo   23 July to 22 August

Symbol: THE LION

Ruling planet: THE SUN

Gender: MASCULINE

Element: FIRE

Quality: FIXED

Yours is a masculine fire sign, so you get on with things quickly. This means you can become irritated at the slow pace that satisfies others.

Some Leo children have a poor relationship with their father or don't see much of him due to his job. These early struggles make you more self-reliant than most other zodiac signs, and you learn to stand on your own feet when you are still young. You might marry early and go on to create your own family unit, and your children soon become the delight of your life. You are a loving partner and a wonderful parent, fairly strict, but always treating your children with dignity. Your faults are bossiness and occasional irritable outbursts (especially when you are tired or hungry).

Ambitious and capable, you reach for the top in whatever line of work you take up. Many of you own your own business. Some of you drift into the world of show business or pop music, where your charisma and dramatic flare help you out. Many Leos succeed in the equally glamorous world of sports or politics. Hard-working and well-organized, it is likely that you will do well in whatever work you take up. You might look grand, want to be in charge, and to be treated like a king or queen, but, in reality, you are just a great big softie who loves to give and receive affection.

The Leo male is at home at the beach as well as in the office. There's nothing he likes more than to relax and read, or watch movies, or television.

Virgo 23 August to 22 September

Symbol: THE MAIDEN

Ruling planet: MERCURY

Gender: FEMININE

Element: EARTH

Quality: MUTABLE

Yours is a feminine earth sign, and while you set about doing things more quickly than the other two earth signs of Taurus and Capricorn, you cannot cope with being rushed.

You are one of the hardest workers of the zodiac, and you have the patience for detail work, but you might shy away from the more stressful kind of executive position. Many of you are drawn to the fields of health and healing, so you might choose to work in established medicine or in alternative healing. Your childhood is likely to have been difficult, and your parents might have behaved toward you in an unnecessarily harsh or critical manner. It is possible you came into their lives at an awkward time and their frustrations spilled over onto you. Soon enough, you leave home to make your own way, and you soon learn that independence and the ability to stand on your own feet is important to your survival. Some of you get into relationships early in life, but these don't always work out too well, and it takes time before you go on to find someone who you can really be happy with.

You take your responsibilities seriously, and your family can rely on you to support them, but you can become so embroiled in your work that you neglect the family on an emotional level.

Your serious nature doesn't prevent you from having fun, and you enjoy vacations and time off doing something that interests you. Your sense of humor, your reliability as a friend, and a kind heart make you a wonderful companion, while excellent communication skills help you keep working.

Caring Virgo can
sometimes forget she
also has a need for
some tender loving
care.

Libra   23 September to 23 October

Symbol: THE SCALES

Ruling planet: VENUS

Gender: MASCULINE

Element: AIR

Quality: CARDINAL

Yours is a masculine air sign, so you like to think, analyze, and study the things that interest you and to talk about them. You can be better at dreaming up ideas and talking about them than you are at getting anything done.

Many of you are absolute masters of tact and diplomacy and a good friend to all who come into contact with you, but there might be a strange sense of detachment or even self-absorption that can make it hard for others to relate fully to you. Your pleasant manner and great sense of humor mean you are always welcome at any social event. Some of you are so charming and flirtatious that you can find yourself being taken seriously by members of the opposite sex when your only real intention is to be pleasant company. You have a talent for seeing all sides of an argument or of a situation, and this makes it difficult for you to come down on one side or another or to choose between two pathways.

Your sign is associated with legal argument, and while it is all right to argue every little point in a courtroom, it can make you difficult to live with. Some Librans are extremely confrontational, which makes them difficult to live or work with.

You enjoy family life as long as it doesn't restrict your freedom. If your partner is the clingy type who insists on interrogating you, you will explode with frustration. If you are happily married, you do your best to make your partner happy and to give your children all that they need. You are eager to see your children succeed in life, and you will sacrifice much to make sure this happens.

Libra's fine sense of balance can make him indecisive at key moments.

Scorpio   24 October to 21 November

Symbol: THE SCORPION

Ruling planet: PLUTO

Gender: FEMININE

Element: WATER

Quality: FIXED

Yours is a feminine water sign, so many of your actions and decisions are taken on the basis of how you feel. You might make decisions instinctively rather than on the basis of pure logic.

You can be very persuasive, which makes you an excellent sales person or counselor, but you must guard against allowing this trait to tip over into manipulative behavior or even a subtle form of bullying or you will lose the advantage you seek. Yours is an all-or-nothing kind of sun sign, so you tend to do everything to excess or not at all. You might drink a lot or you might be a teetotaler—you might spend money freely or be tightfisted. Nobody is more charming and hospitable when you are in the mood for company, but you can be like a bear with a sore head when you are not. Your worst fault is your tendency to criticize others or to feel glee when you see them fall on their face. You are extremely attached to your family, and you will do anything to make sure they are happy, but if a relative gets you down, you can cut them out of your life.

Many of you are drawn to work in the areas of health and healing. This might be in established medicine or in alternative or complementary therapy, and you can be a wonderful psychic healer.

Your instinct is powerful, and you tend to see right to the truth of a matter. You take your career seriously, and you work very hard—often because you don't want to be criticized, or do want to earn respect and approval. Yours is one of the most loyal signs of the zodiac. Once you have made a commitment, you stick to it, and you are the soul of discretion.

Scorpios are the Mr. and Ms. Hospitality of the sun sign world. Here, Ms. Hospitality enjoys a cocktail with Pluto, the sign's ruling planet.

Sagittarius 22 November to 21 December

Symbol: **THE ARCHER**

Ruling planet: **JUPITER**

Gender: **MASCULINE**

Element: **FIRE**

Quality: **MUTABLE**

This is a masculine fire sign. You think and act quickly, and you can see the picture as a whole, but you can have difficulty in handling details.

Sagittarians come in two distinct packages. Some of you are quiet, shy, short of confidence, and only really happy with family or close friends. Others are the most outgoing people in the zodiac. You are a hard worker, and you can be very successful in your career, but occasional lapses of confidence or silly decisions can trip you up or prevent you from reaching your full potential. You often have luck on your side, and you can manage to fall on your feet. Many of you are drawn to astrology and other mystical arts, and you all have a deeply philosophical turn of mind.

You can appear superficial, but you are a deep thinker and can be studious. You love to be on the move and hate to be tied to one place, so you might choose a job that takes you from place to place or a hobby that involves travel.

Sometimes your enthusiastic and optimistic nature urges you to take on more than you can handle. Despite an appearance of great energy, you tire easily and you need time to switch off and give your body and nerves a rest.

You need freedom, so a partner who makes unreasonable demands will soon get you down. Your extreme honesty can make you a little tactless and apt to upset others unwittingly. There is a side to you that never quite grows up, which means you are a fun-loving parent. Sagittarians of both sexes are extremely clever with their hands. You love being outdoors, and you also love to travel and explore, so your family can expect plenty of active vacations.

Bags are packed ready to catch a plane or train out of here! To anywhere! This Sagittarian's taking Jupiter out for a spin.

Capricorn   22 December to 19 January

Symbol: THE GOAT

Ruling planet: SATURN

Gender: MASCULINE

Element: EARTH

Quality: CARDINAL

This feminine earth sign, which denotes practicality, common sense, and attention to detail.

All of you who were born under the sign of Capricorn are ambitious in one way or another, if not for yourself, then for your children. You see to it that your children receive the best education possible and make the most of their opportunities. Being practical, sensible, realistic, and responsible, you take life very seriously, but that doesn't make you humorless or dull because you have a wonderfully dry sense of the ridiculous. You will stay in a job longer than most, even if at times it is hard going.

Quite a few of you are happy to remain single, some due to shyness and awkwardness with the opposite sex, or possibly because you prefer to stay with your parents. When you get into a relationship, you take it very seriously and bend heaven and earth to make it work.

Your faults are fussiness and a tendency to take offense over nothing, and you can sometimes alienate people by your prickly attitude. Some of you might let ambition sweep you over the edge into dubious practices, but most of you tread the straight and narrow path. Business attracts you, with accountancy and banking high on the list. Traditional astrology suggested that the sciences are attached to this house, and these days this can apply to technical knowledge, too.

A large number of you are keen on astrology, psychism, and mystical matters, and equally surprisingly, many of you are good water diviners, wonderful dancers, experts on antiques, winners at some oddball sport, or great cooks.

"You make me feel like dancing" must be a Capricorn's favorite phrase, whatever the time of day. Just put the music on and they're ready to rock 'n' roll.

Aquarius 20 January to 18 February

Symbol: THE WATER CARRIER

Ruling planet: URANUS

Gender: MASCULINE

Element: AIR

Quality: FIXED

This is an air sign, so you are not short of ideas, but you might lack the practicality to put them into action. You can spend more time thinking, researching, or talking than you do getting things done. This is the one sign that beginners always get wrong. Its symbol might be a water carrier, but this has nothing to do with its element, because it is an air sign.

It makes more sense to view the Aquarian pot as a container of ideas instead. Inventive, clever, and often ingenious, you can find a way around problems more successfully than any other sign of the zodiac. You might appear confident, but you actually suffer from shyness and a lack of confidence—though you only let very close loved ones see this. Being kindly and extremely humanitarian, you can become involved in causes. You can take these to extremes or become so wrapped up in world affairs that you might neglect your own family.

Your chief faults are forget-
fulness and not being able to
get anywhere on time.

You are an excellent teacher and have
the world of patience for those who are
willing to learn. You speak slowly and express
yourself clearly, and you always put your ideas
over in a logical and imaginative manner.

Although your appearance is cool and calm, you
are tense inside, and your bottled-up feelings can
explode on occasion into some form of irrational
behavior.

Many of you work in the caring professions,
while many more of you are fascinated by
computers. If you chose a technical job
that has a human side to it, you are
probably in the right career.

You need your family, but you also
need to be independent, so a clingy
partner or highly demanding
children will get you down.
Indeed, many of you avoid
having children altogether.

If your loved one respects
your need to take time out
to pursue your hobbies, you
will be happy.

This is the planet
that tends to turn
everything upside
down, so Aquarians
need to be prepared
for any event.

Pisces   19 February to 20 March

Symbol: THE FISH

Ruling planet: NEPTUNE

Gender: MASCULINE

Element: WATER

Quality: MUTABLE

This is a feminine water sign, so your intuition, feelings, and emotions are at the heart of both your decision-making and actions.

As a Piscean, there is a good chance your life is fairly chaotic, because there is bound to be at least one area of your life you never quite get to grips with. You might have everything nicely buttoned down at work, only to find that your domestic arrangements are in a mess, or you have an organized home life, but a strangely disjointed career. Your house is not a mess, but you

probably have too many interesting objects lying around for neatness. Sometimes, the practicalities of life are easy, but your relationships can be difficult. Your saving grace is that you manage to see the funny side of things, even during the darkest times.

You hate to see people in pain so you rush in to help them, but you must guard against picking up losers who latch on and drain you.

Despite this altruism, you can suddenly become bored by other people's problems and switch off when the need arises. Your intuition is your strongest feature, and it is almost inevitable that you will have an interest in Tarot cards, clairvoyance, and healing.

You are a very loving parent and a hands-on grandparent later in life. Your gentle nature makes you well liked, and you should have no shortage of friends. It is unlikely you will ever become really rich because your values are spiritual rather than material, but you will always have what you need.

Neptune rules this sign, but even planets need an occasional bit of advice from a Pisces.

Living with

This chapter sets out to demystify the role that the planets play in your everyday life.

planets

The Sun

Even though on first acquaintance, your rising sign is what others are most likely to spot, your sun sign will be important, because it is always there at the heart of you. Your sun sign is the only planetary position you are sure to know about without studying astrology at all. Even those who don't appear on the face of things to be much like their sun sign will have the essentials of its character somewhere around.

So, an apparently wimpy fire person will fight like a tiger for what he or she thinks is right. An outwardly chaotic earth person will never be stupid where financial necessities are concerned. A seemingly dull air person has a mind that is always active. A quiet, dry water person will always be able to rely upon a powerful inner world of imagination and intuition.

THE SUN IN THE SIGNS AND HOUSES

ARIES first house	TAURUS second house	GEMINI third house	CANCER fourth house	LEO fifth house	VIRGO sixth house
Idealistic, self-motivated, unable to tolerate fools, needs a meaningful career, headstrong	Cautious with money, a real family person, needs security, resists change, materialistic	Quick on the uptake, needs variety at work, good communicator, good parent, can whine	Good homemaker and family person, needs a calm atmosphere in the home, shrewd, emotional, moody, and possessive	Loyal, has high personal standards and leadership qualities, has zest for life, can be arrogant, irritable, and bossy	Copes well with details, good friend, great sense of humor, needs emotional support

SUN DATA

- the sun is about 93 million miles (150 kilometers) from earth
- it is so vast that you could fit 109 earths inside it
- the sun is actually a star but astrologers use it as a planet
- it is at the center of the system of planets that earth belongs to

Your sun sign energy is at the heart of your sign, so it will be a great influence on your nature.

LIBRA seventh house	**SCORPIO** eighth house	**SAGITTARIUS** ninth house	**CAPRICORN** tenth house	**AQUARIUS** eleventh house	**PISCES** twelfth house
Sociable and friendly, refined and artistic, good homemaker, but can be argumentative	Tenacious, loyal to family and friends, persuasive, feels deeply, can have a hot temper, or be moody and possessive	Quick minded, dexterous, restless, optimistic, sensitive, kind, sometimes lacks common sense	Sensible, businesslike, ambitious, good to parents and family, can be unsociable	Original and inventive mind, broadminded, humanitarian, good teacher, can be vague and forgetful	Sociable and friendly, cares for less fortunate people, artistic, mystical, psychic, sometimes sharp-tongued or moody

The Moon

he moon represents your inner, hidden, and emotional nature, and it rules the kind of behavior you fall back on when instinct and habit take over. Your moon sign and house can show your real motives and ambitions. The moon relates to mother figures and the kind of nurturing you received. It also concerns the past, either your own past or an interest in history. The moon is the "domestic" planet, so it signifies your home and tic circumstances, and reflects your attitude to family life. When you look through the checklists below, don't confine yourself to your own sun sign—check them all.

You might discover you have more in common with some other sign, and that can turn out to be your rising sign, your moon sign, or a place where a bunch of planets congregated on the day of your birth.

MOON DATA

- earth's only natural satellite
- diameter of 2,160 miles (3,476 km), a quarter that of the earth
- circles earth every 27 days, 7 hours, 43 minutes, and 11 seconds
- illuminated by the sun
- a full moon always rises at sunset and sets at sunrise
- does not have any air or liquid water

THE MOON IN THE SIGNS AND HOUSES

ARIES first house	TAURUS second house	GEMINI third house	CANCER fourth house	LEO fifth house	VIRGO sixth house
Ambitious, self-motivated, self-centered	Security conscious, materialistic, comfort-loving	Humorous, intelligent, a worrier	Good teacher, family-minded, might be close to mother	Childish, creative, loves drama, self-centered	Health conscious, analytical mind, can have a critical mother

Your moon sign makes you reach out for love and understanding, but those with the moon in fire and air signs also need their independence.

LIBRA
seventh house

Tasteful, likes companionship but fears commitment

SCORPIO
eighth house

Intense feelings, intelligent, critical, often psychic

SAGITTARIUS
ninth house

Needs emotional freedom, broad-minded, might have a whacky mother

CAPRICORN
tenth house

Ambitious, self-sufficient, might have harsh parents

AQUARIUS
eleventh house

Friendly, humanitarian, intelligent, can be eccentric

PISCES
twelfth house

Religious or mystical, intuitive, vulnerable, gentle

Mercury

This fast-moving planet is associated with the ability to communicate as well as with the modern machinery used for communicating with each other. Mercury also concerns your relationships with sisters, brothers, friends, relatives of your own age, and your neighbors. It relates to neighborhood matters and the way you get around the local area.

MERCURY DATA

- first planet from the sun at never more than 27 degrees away.
- diameter of 3,030 miles (4,880 km)
- orbits sun in 88 days
- known as an "inferior" planet
- floats low in the sky, making it difficult to see
- covered in craters
- very hot on one side, cold on the other side

MERCURY IN THE SIGNS AND HOUSES

ARIES first house	TAURUS second house	GEMINI third house	CANCER fourth house	LEO fifth house	VIRGO sixth house
Quick thinking, active, competitive, sporty	Thorough and capable, clever with finances	Quick thinking, great communicator, always up to date with what's happening	Might work from home, may marry a relative	Good at games and business, well organized	Logical, analytical, clever, might be fussy, health-conscious

When Mercury is moving in an awkward manner, misunderstandings occur and important pieces of paper get lost. Due to this planet's close proximity to the sun, it is located either in the same sign as your sun, or in the one that comes immediately before or after it.

LIBRA **seventh house**	**SCORPIO** **eighth house**	**SAGITTARIUS** **ninth house**	**CAPRICORN** **tenth house**	**AQUARIUS** **eleventh house**	**PISCES** **twelfth house**
Attracted to the arts, good agent, needs a companion to talk to	Deep, quick mind, good investigator, interested in mental or physical health	Broad-minded, good with hands, enjoys travel	Slow but thorough thinker, banking, business, and money appeal	Original mind, inventive, has quirky friends who are a lot of fun	Great ideas—but are they practical? Highly psychic people

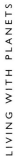

Venus

Venus relates to the things you possess and value, not necessarily money, but anything of importance to you, such things as a collection of ornaments, shelves of books, your partner in life, and personal freedom. Venus shows the way you give love and what you want from a lover. It is the planet of luxury, relaxation, and having a good time, but it also rules open enemies.

VENUS DATA

- second planet from the sun
- 7,500 miles (12,100 km) in diameter, slightly less than earth
- brightest object in the sky after the sun and the moon
- covered in bright clouds
- spins on its axis from east to west, the opposite direction from most other planets
- always seen close to the sun in the sky at twilight or dawn
- located 67 million miles (108 million km) from the sun

VENUS IN THE SIGNS AND HOUSES

ARIES first house	TAURUS second house	GEMINI third house	CANCER fourth house	LEO fifth house	VIRGO sixth house
Own needs count over others' needs, can be possessive	Sensuality, a love of beauty, have some kind of creative talent	Books, ideas, contact with others, friendships may be easier than relationships	Great homemaker, enjoys the family, close to the mother	Children, lovers, fun, music; creative outlet is vital	Books, productive work; loyal but not possessive

When Venus is in its own signs of Taurus and Libra, people can have a penchant for shopping for clothes and household accessories. People under both signs usually have an artistic talent and dress well.

LIBRA seventh house	**SCORPIO** eighth house	**SAGITTARIUS** ninth house	**CAPRICORN** tenth house	**AQUARIUS** eleventh house	**PISCES** twelfth house
Love, luxury, pleasure, beauty, a need for justice	Very possessive, passionate and deep; money vital for happiness	Personal freedom is vital, values truth and new ideas	Ambitious, materialistic, values achievement	Friendship with influential people, education is important	Art, music, creativity, mystical matters, love matters

Mars

This planet shows how you go after what you want, and it expresses the assertive, masculine side of your nature. It can show the way you act when you are attracted to someone and what you do to obtain love and sex. Mars shows how you use your energy and for what purpose, including what you fight for and the way you go about it.

MARS DATA

- fourth planet from the sun
- diameter of 4,222 miles (6,794 km), slightly more than half the earth's diameter
- has a 24-hour day and a series of seasons like earth's
- has polar ice caps since the temperature rarely rises above freezing
- called the Red Planet because it is covered in red deserts
- circles the sun once every 687 days
- has two small moons called Phobos and Deimos

MARS IN THE SIGNS AND HOUSES

ARIES first house	TAURUS second house	GEMINI third house	CANCER fourth house	LEO fifth house	VIRGO sixth house
Decisive, active, pioneering, sexy, accident prone	Thorough, able to finish what is started, creative	Talkative, intelligent, will work with computers, or as a communicator	Good at do-it-yourself, will put energy into family life—a wimp!	Salesmanship, hard worker, charismatic, childish	Hard worker, good mind, can be talkative

Mars in Scorpio can make someone behave in a secretive way! If Mars is in a fire sign, the person is likely to be competitive, making them good at sporting activities. Mars in other signs doesn't imply weakness, but it indicates other things are more important than winning!

LIBRA seventh house	**SCORPIO** eighth house	**SAGITTARIUS** ninth house	**CAPRICORN** tenth house	**AQUARIUS** eleventh house	**PISCES** twelfth house
A great lover, materialistic, loves luxury	Very sexy, intense, possessive, can be secretive	Religion and philosophy, good at sports, enjoys traveling	Ambitious, hard worker, clever; likely to be a scientist or mathematician	Good student or teacher; friendly, humanitarian	Creative, romantic, good swimmer; can be a dreamer

Jupiter

The sign and house that Jupiter occupies will throw considerable light on your beliefs and your value system. It also determines how adventurous you are and the way you attempt to expand your horizons. Jupiter in some signs inclines the person to be a risk-taker; in others it breathes life into what might otherwise be a dull personality. Jupiter defines how you are likely to find luck. This planet rules higher education, philosophy, legal and political argument, and travel.

JUPITER DATA

- fifth planet from the sun
- diameter of 88,850 miles (143,000 km)
- largest planet in the solar system
- weighs twice as much as other planets
- orbits sun once every 11.9 years
- composed mainly of gas
- its four largest moons were first seen in 1610 by Galileo Galilei

JUPITER IN THE SIGNS AND HOUSES

ARIES first house	TAURUS second house	GEMINI third house	CANCER fourth house	LEO fifth house	VIRGO sixth house
Strong beliefs, love of truth, love of travel, self-motivation	Legal or spiritual work can provide a living, may overspend	Talking or writing will bring luck and money	A wealthy background perhaps, or luck through property	Creative work and children bring luck; lucky winner but can be a big spender	Work brings luck, original ideas can also prove lucky

Jupiter is said to be the lucky planet. When in Sagittarius, the first or the tenth houses, it can help you to get out of trouble. When in the seventh, eighth, tenth, or eleventh houses, other people will help get you out of trouble!

LIBRA seventh house	**SCORPIO** eighth house	**SAGITTARIUS** ninth house	**CAPRICORN** tenth house	**AQUARIUS** eleventh house	**PISCES** twelfth house
Luck through marriage or partnerships	Legacies, marriage, or divorce bring luck	Travel and exploration are lucky, spiritual matters also fascinate	Success in science or politics, career advancement also likely	Luck comes in unusual ways or through friends	Your values are spiritual rather than material, so luck cannot be counted in money

Saturn

Dour old Saturn is the planet all student astrologers (especially wimps) love to hate. It represents restrictions and limitations,

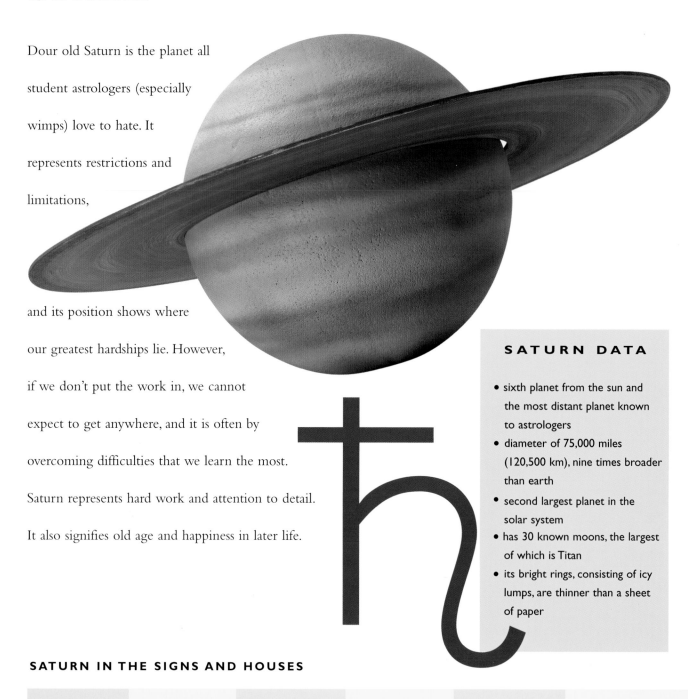

and its position shows where our greatest hardships lie. However, if we don't put the work in, we cannot expect to get anywhere, and it is often by overcoming difficulties that we learn the most. Saturn represents hard work and attention to detail. It also signifies old age and happiness in later life.

SATURN DATA

- sixth planet from the sun and the most distant planet known to astrologers
- diameter of 75,000 miles (120,500 km), nine times broader than earth
- second largest planet in the solar system
- has 30 known moons, the largest of which is Titan
- its bright rings, consisting of icy lumps, are thinner than a sheet of paper

SATURN IN THE SIGNS AND HOUSES

ARIES first house	TAURUS second house	GEMINI third house	CANCER fourth house	LEO fifth house	VIRGO sixth house
A difficult early life, but hard work pays off later	It takes time to accumulate money and possessions, plenty of common sense	Early education is poor or unpleasant, success later through writing	Stressful early life, difficult parents, good home life later	Children might be a burden, can work too hard	Much work and sacrifice on behalf of others, possible poor health

Some astrologers consider Saturn to represent the father on a chart, while others say it is the mother. Saturn actually symbolizes any person who sets boundaries, shows how to keep out of harm's way, and teaches how to fit into society. This planet also rules clocks, calendars, and measuring tools.

LIBRA seventh house	**SCORPIO** eighth house	**SAGITTARIUS** ninth house	**CAPRICORN** tenth house	**AQUARIUS** eleventh house	**PISCES** twelfth house
Marriage to a much older or younger partner	Success in business and with finances after a tough start	Must guard against being too opinionated, travel for business and fame far from home	A tough start, but fame and success at last, strong parents	Friends might influence your career—or use you	One of your parents was difficult, avoid lame ducks

Uranus

Uranus is the "breakout" planet. It breaks the rules and causes upheavals in our lives. In a birth chart, Uranus rules creativity, originality, and sometimes psychic gifts. It is associated with higher education, science, new invention, and new ideas. It also rules friendship and other detached relationships, political ideas, and personal freedom.

URANUS DATA

- seventh planet from the sun
- diameter of 31,800 miles (51,100 km), four times that of the earth
- orbits sun once every 84 years
- third-largest planet in the solar system
- discovered in 1781 by British astronomer William Herschel
- seems to orbit the sun on its side

URANUS IN THE SIGNS AND HOUSES

ARIES first house	TAURUS second house	GEMINI third house	CANCER fourth house	LEO fifth house	VIRGO sixth house
Rebellious, independent, or eccentric, friendships important	Fluctuations in goods, money, and possessions, unusual talents	An unusual or disrupted education, talent for communicating	Unusual family or home circumstances	Gifted children, unusual talents, lucky at gambling or sports	Might have two jobs or unusual interests, talented

Uranus is said to rule friends and friendship, but this planet also refers to those people whose influence will help you to get on in life.

LIBRA seventh house	**SCORPIO** eighth house	**SAGITTARIUS** ninth house	**CAPRICORN** tenth house	**AQUARIUS** eleventh house	**PISCES** twelfth house
Several marriages, ups and downs in life due to partnerships	Sudden gains and losses due to events that concern others	May marry a foreigner or travel to strange places, has many friends	Unusual career or dual careers, good teacher, interested in politics	Many friends, wide-ranging interests, could be an astrologer	Intuitive, psychic, artistic, musical, unusual lifestyle and friends

Neptune

Neptune is associated with the sea and with travel, but also with dreams, imagination, creativity, and escape from humdrum life. It relates to psychic matters, intuition, mysticism, religion and spiritual ideas, as well as art, music, and all that makes life pleasant. There is a dark side, however, that makes it difficult for us to see what's what on occasion, and it can cause muddles, swindles, misunderstandings, illusions, and delusions. This is the planet of escapist behavior and drunkenness. Neptune is hard to explain or understand—but that is probably a deliberate ploy!

NEPTUNE DATA

- eighth planet from the sun
- diameter of 30, 800 miles (49,500 km), four times wider than earth
- orbits sun once every 165 years
- has at least eight moons, the largest of which is Triton
- atmosphere rich in hydrogen, helium, and methane
- discovered in 1846
- invisible to the naked eye

NEPTUNE IN THE SIGNS AND HOUSES

ARIES first house	TAURUS second house	GEMINI third house	CANCER fourth house	LEO fifth house	VIRGO sixth house
Creative, artistic, might never get their act together	Strange ups and downs regarding wealth and possessions	Clever with words, can be a medium, work and education unstable	Home life is confusing, and family might not be sane or sober	Talented, sensitive children, but it is hard to provide stability for them	Attracted to work in health or healing, strong social conscience

Neptune is sometimes referred to as the planet of self-undoing! There are times when we shoot ourselves in the foot (Neptune rules the feet), and when this happens we can be sure Neptune is up to no good on the horoscope front.

LIBRA seventh house	**SCORPIO** eighth house	**SAGITTARIUS** ninth house	**CAPRICORN** tenth house	**AQUARIUS** eleventh house	**PISCES** twelfth house
Very happy or miserable in relationships, must avoid rescuing lame dogs	Money comes and goes, depending on the actions of others	Travel over water or a home by the sea brings luck and peace	Can work in an artistic, musical, or spiritual field	Oddball friends bring inspiration and fun	Very artistic and dreamy, but needs to keep track of reality

Pluto

Pluto rules transformation, even to the point of destroying a life so it can be rebuilt in a better way later. It is associated with union and dependent partnerships, so it is associated with shared resources, big money, and such things as taxes, mortgages, and legacies. Union can also imply sexual relationships and the major family issues of birth, death, gains, and losses.

PLUTO DATA

- ninth planet from the sun
- orbits sun once every 248 years
- diameter of 1,430 miles (2,300 km), two-thirds of the moon's
- smallest of all planets
- discovered in 1930 by astronomer Clyde Tombaugh

PLUTO IN THE SIGNS AND HOUSES

ARIES **first house**	**TAURUS** **second house**	**GEMINI** **third house**	**CANCER** **fourth house**	**LEO** **fifth house**	**VIRGO** **sixth house**
Politician or leader with power for good or ill	Can become extremely wealthy—or lose everything	Wonderful communicator, you can make money from writing	Powerful family, for good or ill, the past exerts a strong hold	Children or enterprises transform your life	Can achieve much on behalf of others, can be a workaholic

The transforming effect of Pluto takes time to come about, so when something happens to upset our lives it can take a while for us to rebuild. Learning to overcome problems can be difficult at the time, but these experiences are part of life and they help us develop as a person.

LIBRA
seventh house

Marriage can bring great gains or losses

SCORPIO
eighth house

Legacies, mortgages, tax, corporate matters, and marriage bring luck or losses

SAGITTARIUS
ninth house

Wish to improve the world, foreign ventures or immigration bring money

CAPRICORN
tenth house

Public success and a power, but setbacks are possible

AQUARIUS
eleventh house

New and revolutionary ideas bring success, powerful friends are helpful

PISCES
twelfth house

Very psychic, good healer, painful life, but eager to help others

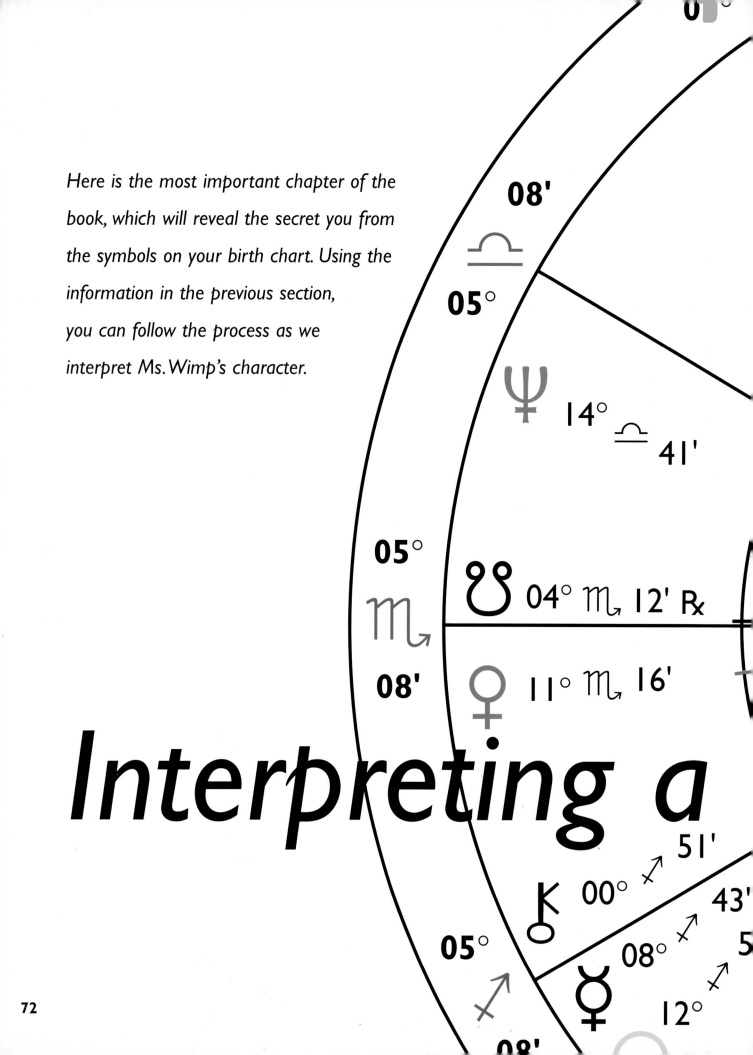

Here is the most important chapter of the book, which will reveal the secret you from the symbols on your birth chart. Using the information in the previous section, you can follow the process as we interpret Ms. Wimp's character.

08'

♎︎

05°

♆ 14° ♎︎ 41'

05°

♏︎

08'

☋ 04° ♏︎ 12' ℞

♀ 11° ♏︎ 16'

Interpreting a

51'

⚷ 00° ♐︎

43'

08° ♐︎

05°

♐︎

☿ 12°

08'

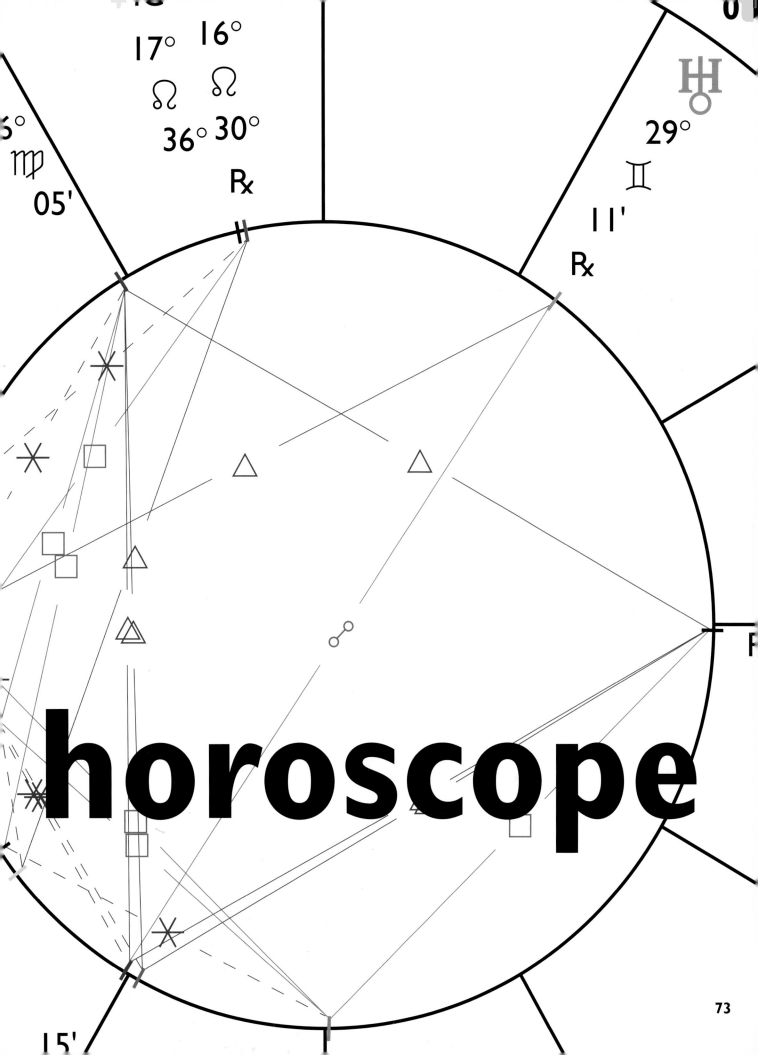

horoscope

Creating a horoscope

Here, I introduce a character I call Ms. Wimp. I picked a random date, so she is a fictitious person who could only really be exactly like someone who was born at the same time, on the same day, and in the same place. Ms. Wimp was born in Santa Monica, California, on April 2, 1972, at 16:25 PST.

MS. WIMP'S COMPUTER-GENERATED BIRTH CHART

Mercury and Venus are close to the sun and usually in the same sign as the sun. Her sun and Mercury are in Aries, but Venus is in Taurus. In her case, Venus is a fair distance from the sun, which is unusual.

How to work out your chart

There are still some astrology students and astrologers who know how to work out a chart entirely by hand, but this process has been eclipsed by the easy accessibility of excellent software at reasonable prices. You can download software packages directly online, or buy them in any reputable astrology store. Even top astrology schools no longer teach students how to do it by hand!

There are many websites devoted to astrology. Find one that will give you up to four free charts so you can start to interpret the various signs.

Here, we examine the characteristics revealed in a computer chart, using Ms. Wimp as an example. Her chart was drawn up using Solar Fire software. To show you how to create a chart by hand, I would have had to attach a math primer, a calculator, a new brain, and all of this would have been enough to make a wimp weep.

The wimp's way to draw up a chart is by computer. The wimp's way to interpret what is generated is easy once you know how from what I am about to show you.

If you want to experiment with computerized charts, log on to www.astro.com and use their service. This site lets you generate up to four charts absolutely free of charge. After this you will find it easy to transfer to any system because they all require the same information: the person's name, plus their date, time, and place of birth.

As a professional astrologer I use a variety of software, not just this package. There is a wide choice of software to buy, however, the packages differ in what they offer. As a beginner you need software that will give you a chart, and a report, which is an interpretation of what everything means. The best way is to ask among your astrologer friends and people working in the store to see what you get for your money.

Ms. Wimp's rising sign

Here you will learn how to read the rising sign, the sign that was rising over the horizon at the time of birth. It is an influential feature on any chart, especially Ms. Wimp's.

Look at Ms. Wimp's chart on the previous page and find this section. This indicates the rising sign, which is at 20 degrees 54 minutes into Virgo. The colored section indicates her first house, which runs from 20 degrees 54 minutes Virgo to the same point in Libra.

The rising sign is the first thing to look for and it opens the door to the chart. It is a revelation! In this case, it shows us the kinds of experiences she had as a child, what her parents taught her and expected of her and the lessons she picked up from school, friends, and the society she lived in from birth to her teenage years.

It is the strongest key to the impressions she would have gained as a child. In her case, a highly disciplined childhood, one where she was brought up to please others, to behave properly, and to fit in without making waves. Her individuality and creativity were low on the agenda of those immediately around her, so she would have had to discover these within herself later in life.

This childhood would not have worried her unduly—she would have respected her parents and done as they wished, even though it may have seemed repressive at times. She would have bitten her tongue and kept her own counsel.

Being an Aries, she would have bounced up and out of the restrictive environment at home in her teenage years.

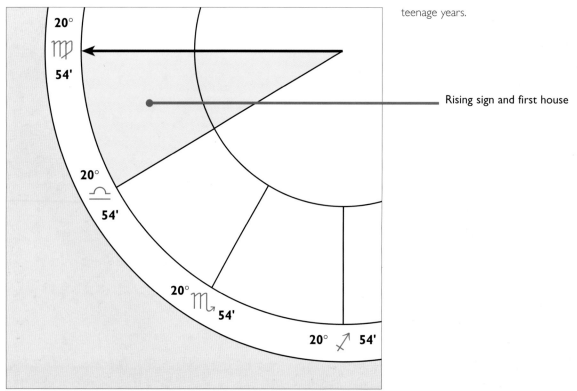

Rising sign and first house

THE MIDHEAVEN

At the top of the chart you can see her midheaven is in Gemini. This location will help her achieve the cool, centered, intellectual goals she so desires, and to grow into herself so she is not a victim or an emotional wimp!

It allows her to communicate her ideas, and confirms that teaching is her best career choice, but gives her the ability to connect with others, and to have her ideas taken on board. It may add to her touch of fame when her writing, broadcasting, and singing hobbies take off.

She must try not to let the men in her life take advantage of her, and learn to negotiate quietly, firmly, and unemotionally for what she wants.

Midheaven in Gemini

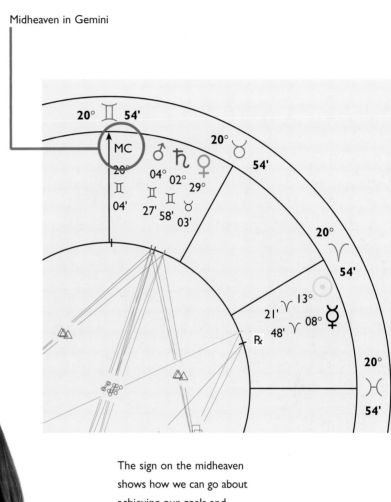

The sign on the midheaven shows how we can go about achieving our goals and objectives. In Ms. Wimp's case, Gemini at the midheaven says communication is the key to success.

Why does the rising sign matter?

The rising sign matters for two reasons. The first is that it is the starting point for the 12 astrological houses that run round the chart in a counterclockwise direction from the ascendant. The second is that it gives a wealth of information about the kind of background, childhood, and programming each of us received when young. People often act and look more like their rising sign than their sun sign. Following are the indications of each rising sign for you to learn.

Ms. Wimp's rising sign is Virgo. Her creativity came to the fore once she left her teenage years and became an adult.

ARIES RISING

A parent might be unreasonable, and confrontations occur when the child reaches the teen years and the child can escape by leaving home when young. Some opt for life in the armed forces, and others create a home and family while young. Adults are quiet and introspective.

TAURUS RISING

Something is askew in childhood, which might make financial security or financial independence imperative. There is a practical streak combined with creative talent and humor, but the adult can be argumentative.

GEMINI RISING

The childhood is often lonely and hard, and even if the home life was reasonable, this person will have felt alienated elsewhere. These children are talkative, and adults don't want to listen, or deliberately misunderstand them. Adults of this sign become communicators and writers, but they never really become confident.

CANCER RISING

The mother is a strong influence, either being deeply loving or powerful and frightening. This child has a responsible attitude, and might later marry a younger partner, or one who is insecure or who needs mothering. There is shrewdness and good business sense.

LEO RISING

This child is considered special, either due to talent or sometimes for no discernable reason. There is a desire for glamour, an interest in performing, and a need to be the center of attention. The person will be a loving parent, but possibly somewhat vain.

VIRGO RISING

The mother is highly critical and disapproving—she may not actually like the child. There is great emphasis on outer behavior, school achievements, and what the neighbors think. The adult lacks self-confidence and feels undeserving.

LIBRA RISING

The father may have been absent during childhood or switched off from family life. The child can be indulged with possessions, but real needs might be neglected. As an adult, the person is attractive and charming, but possibly self-indulgent.

SCORPIO RISING

The child is loved, but there are outside circumstances that make life difficult, and the person feels out of step with others. This breeds a cautious attitude, secrecy, and intense feelings that are kept hidden. As an adult, privacy is valued, and psychic, psychological, or medical matters might be investigated.

SAGITTARIUS RISING

There is a desire to leave home early and to experiment with ideas and philosophies. The parents might be foreigners, or the child might emigrate or change cultures. The mind is keen, and the values are spiritual rather than materialistic.

CAPRICORN RISING

This signifies a hard childhood, but this isn't due to bad parents. There may be a large family, poverty, or bereavement. Money, security, and a decent career become important. The person becomes ambitious, serious, and a little too hard on themselves or on others.

AQUARIUS RISING

This person learns to be independent early, either through necessity or parental encouragement. The childhood is either very good or extremely unhappy. As an adult, they go their own way and might take an interest in unusual subjects.

PISCES RISING

There is a measure of pain and loneliness in childhood. The parents can be ineffective, so the child learns early to cope. Later, the person combines common sense with intuition to become a success. As an adult, they can be either charming, or extremely prickly.

The astrological houses

The rising sign is the starting point for the 12 houses. The first house starts at the exact

degree of the sign that's rising. On the computer-generated chart, you will see Ms. Wimp's

ascendant is actually well into the sign of Virgo, which is the start of her first house. Look

at the listing for the first house on the opposite page to see what the first house tells you

about her.

MS. WIMP'S CHART SHOWING THE SIGNS AND HOUSES

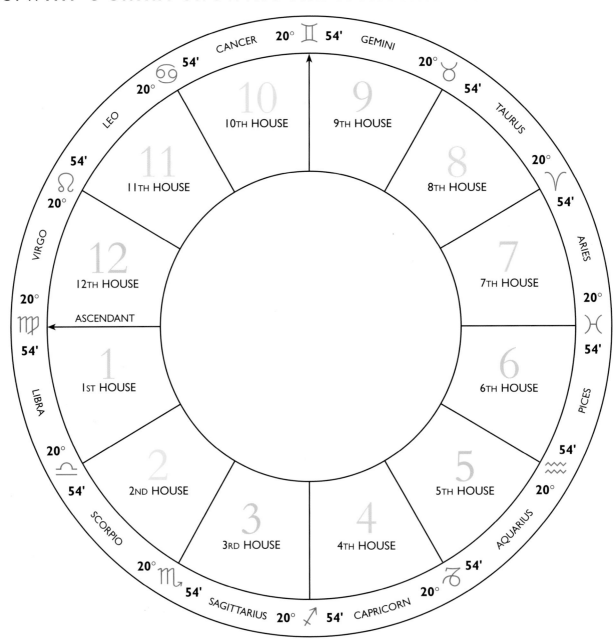

THE HOUSES

Firstly, it is important to know that there are 30 degrees to each sign, all 12 signs making up the 360 degrees that are in the circle. Each sign starts at 0 degrees and ends at 29 degrees.

The starting point for the houses is the degree within the rising sign that is coming up over the horizon at the time of the person's birth. This is called the ascendant.

If the ascendant is near the beginning of the rising sign, most of that sign will also form the first house. For example, if someone had 2 degrees into the sign of Scorpio rising, most of Scorpio would be in the first house.

If the ascendant is later in the sign, as in Ms. Wimp's case, that sign will still exert a strong influence. When the ascendant is close to the very end of the sign, the sign still has some influence, but the fact that the next sign along occupies much of the first house also needs to be taken into consideration.

Look through the characteristics of each house listed and keep them in mind when you are reading a person's chart.

THE FIRST HOUSE

The first house emphasizes childhood programming. This sign may rule your appearance, manner, and some health issues. It can show talents and perhaps the career or lifestyle that suits the person.

THE SECOND HOUSE

Values, including personal possessions and personal finances, your basic security needs, self-esteem, and the way you are valued by others. Abstract priorities such as time, security, love, and freedom.

THE THIRD HOUSE

Siblings, neighbors, and close friendships, also communications, information, and figure work. The mentality, basic education, and level of dexterity are shown here. This house rules local travel, short journeys and your mode of transportation.

THE FOURTH HOUSE

Mother-figures, the childhood home, and domestic circumstances throughout your life, including your home, land, property, or business premises. Mainly family matters, but also the past, antiques, history, and patriotism.

THE FIFTH HOUSE

Artistry and the ability to create. This can apply to raising children, a business enterprise, or a work of art. Also, pleasure, vacation, hobbies, and games for fun. Sometimes love affairs and any other kind of break from routine.

THE SIXTH HOUSE

Employers and employees, work and duty of all kinds. Health, prevention of illness, and anything to do with fitness are indicated here.

THE SEVENTH HOUSE

Traditionally, the house of marriage, but any close partnership that is above board, including business partnerships. Also agreements, contracts, and justice. Open relationships can include enemies!

THE EIGHTH HOUSE

Shared finances and resources, either personal or business. It rules dealings with financial institutions, legacies, taxes, corporate matters, and even the police or judiciary. Birth, death, sex, and karma are associated with this house, as are secrets, resentment, pain, transformation, and hidden or occult matters.

THE NINTH HOUSE

Long-distance travel, foreigners, foreign goods, or different cultures, also issues of freedom, independence, and exploration. Anything that expands intellectual horizons, such as education, religion or philosophy, and justice. Also gambling and luck.

THE TENTH HOUSE

This represents any goal or ambition. Authority figures, especially father figures, are here. Also, status, public acclaim, political advancement, and anything outside the home or in the public gaze.

THE ELEVENTH HOUSE

Detached relationships, clubs, societies, and group activities. The acquisition of knowledge and original or unusual ideas are here, as are intellectual pastimes and astrology. Also unpredictable or slightly off-beat matters.

THE TWELFTH HOUSE

This house rules sacrifice and caring for the weak, places of seclusion, such as prisons and hospitals, or even working quietly at home. Also mysticism, things that are hidden, secrets, and feelings of insecurity. This can lend artistry, musical talent, or psychic ability.

Find the moon

Ms. Wimp's full chart shows the exact position of the moon in her chart. The moon-finder on this page will allow you to find her moon without the aid of a computer! It's a bit of fun, and you will be able to follow the same process to find yours. However, the position will not be exact, but it will be good enough for you to work out certain characteristics.

YEAR					MONTH											
					JAN	FEB	MAR	APR	MAY	JUNE	JULY	AUG	SEP	OCT	NOV	DEC
1920	1939	1958	1977	1996	Tau	Can	Can	Vir	Lib	Sag	Cap	Aqu	Ari	Tau	Can	Leo
1921	1940	1959	1978	1997	Lib	Sco	Sag	Cap	Aqu	Ari	Tau	Can	Leo	Vir	Sco	Sag
1922	1941	1960	1979	1998	Aqu	Ari	Ari	Gem	Can	Leo	Vir	Sco	Cap	Aqu	Ari	Tau
1923	1942	1961	1980	2000	Gem	Leo	Leo	Lib	Sco	Cap	Aqu	Ari	Tau	Gem	Leo	Vir
1924	1943	1962	1981	2001	Sco	Sag	Cap	Aqu	Ari	Tau	Gem	Leo	Lib	Sco	Sag	Cap
1925	1944	1963	1982	2002	Pis	Tau	Tau	Can	Leo	Lib	Sco	Sag	Aqu	Pis	Tau	Gem
1926	1945	1964	1983	2003	Leo	Vir	Lib	Sco	Sag	Aqu	Pis	Tau	Can	Leo	Vir	Lib
1927	1946	1965	1984	2004	Sag	Cap	Aqu	Pis	Tau	Gem	Leo	Vir	Sco	Sag	Aqu	Pis
1928	1947	1966	1985	2005	Ari	Gem	Gem	Leo	Vir	Sco	Sag	Aqu	Pis	Ari	Gem	Can
1929	1948	1967	1986	2006	Vir	Sco	Sco	Cap	Aqu	Pis	Tau	Gem	Leo	Vir	Lib	Sag
1930	1949	1968	1987	2007	Cap	Pis	Pis	Tau	Gem	Leo	Vir	Sco	Sag	Cap	Pis	Ari
1931	1950	1969	1988	2008	Tau	Can	Can	Vir	Lib	Sag	Cap	Pis	Ari	Gem	Can	Leo
1932	1951	1970	1989	2009	Lib	Sag	Sag	Aqu	Pis	Tau	Gem	Can	Vir	Lib	Sag	Cap
1933	1952	1971	1990	2010	Pis	Ari	Tau	Gem	Can	Vir	Lib	Sag	Cap	Aqu	Ari	Tau
1934	1953	(1972)	1991	2011	Can	Vir	Vir	(Lib)	Sag	Cap	Pis	Ari	Gem	Can	Vir	Lib
1935	1954	1973	1992		Sco	Cap	Cap	Pis	Ari	Gem	Can	Vir	Sco	Sag	Cap	Aqu
1936	1955	1974	1993		Ari	Tau	Gem	Leo	Vir	Lib	Sco	Cap	Pis	Ari	Tau	Can
1937	1956	1975	1994		Leo	Lib	Lib	Sag	Cap	Pis	Ari	Tau	Can	Leo	Lib	Sco
1938	1957	1976	1995		Cap	Aqu	Pis	Ari	Tau	Can	Leo	Lib	Sco	Cap	Aqu	Ari

FINDING YOUR MOON SIGN

1

Go to the large table on page 82.
In the section on the left, headed YEAR
find Ms. Wimp's year of birth—1972.

2

In the same table, go to the section on the right,
headed MONTH, track along the same line to
Ms. Wimp's birth month—April. Her moon sign is
listed as Lib, for Libra.

3

Now look at the table on this page, headed
EXACT DAY OF BIRTH. Find the 2nd for Ms.
Wimp, and note the number under it, which is the
number 1. This tells you to move one sign along
from Libra, which is Scorpio. Ms. Wimp's moon sign
is Scorpio.

Ms. Wimp's date of birth : April 2, 1972

$$\text{♎} + 1 = \text{♏}$$

4

Check with the computerized
chart to find her moon, which
is in Scorpio, in the very last
degree of that sign.

EXACT DAY OF BIRTH

1	2	3	4	5	6	7	8
0	1	1	1	2	2	3	3
9	10	11	12	13	14	15	16
4	4	5	5	5	6	6	7
17	18	19	20	21	22	23	24
7	8	8	9	9	10	10	10
25	26	27	28	29	30	31	
11	11	12	12	1	1	2	

 Aries

 Taurus

 Gemini

 Cancer

 Leo

 Virgo

 Libra

 Scorpio

 Sagittarius

 Capricorn

 Aquarius

Pisces

Moon sign characteristics

MOON IN ARIES

You think and talk quickly, and you can cope with large-scale plans, although you might need help when it comes to actually getting things done. Your enthusiasm and energy need a career that is meaningful to you. If you are a woman, being a homemaker will not be enough.

You might have a stormy love life categorized by arguments, due to your inability to compromise or to allow anyone else to dictate to you. Your emotions are quick to surface, and you have a temper, but you can just as easily be warm and loving—and your sex drive is high.

MOON IN TAURUS

You are only stable and happy when your life is in perfect working order. You can deal with practical problems efficiently, but emotional problems upset you. You have a pleasant, friendly, sociable manner, and you are reliable and decent, but you can be self-absorbed or clannish. Your mother exerts a powerful force on you for good or bad.

You have a sensual nature that endows a love of music, flowers, nature, the outdoors, and traveling. You can be stubborn or apt to see things from your own point of view, but you are loving, reliable, and consistent. You need money in the bank and a roof over your head, and will work hard to provide these things for yourself and your family.

MOON IN GEMINI

You have an active and logical mind, and you can turn your hand to anything when the need arises. You love to read and travel. Oddly enough for such a bright person, you might not have achieved much at school, possibly because you were a little different from your peer group. Your adult friendships can only be superficial until other people prove themselves to you. You can hold some part of yourself back emotionally, even when in a love relationship. You will make sure your children receive the best education you can afford, and you will find it easy to talk to them. Being a worker, you can always earn money when the need arises.

Ms. Wimp has the moon in Scorpio, making her secretive on occasions.

MOON IN CANCER

You are emotional, sensitive, and moody, although you seek to hide this from outsiders. You can be imaginative and creative, and you certainly appreciate music and the arts. Being naturally intuitive, you can be drawn to psychic or mystical matters, but you can be equally at home in teaching or business.

You are a good family member and an excellent parent, being reasonably domesticated. Shyness and nervousness may make you suspicious of strangers, but once you make a friend or commit yourself, you do so wholeheartedly. You have a kind heart, but you can be moody.

MOON IN LEO

You can be genuinely confident or able to put on a display of confidence when it is needed. Admiration is important to you, as is being the center of attention. Being an excellent organizer means you can take advantage of trends and opportunities as they arise.

You are not keen on your own company, so you soon make new friends and lovers. In a settled relationship, you can put your partner on a pedestal, and you will certainly do this with your children. Some of you might want to be the child in a relationship.

THE MOON IN VIRGO

You try to control your emotions, but they have a nasty habit of breaking through just when you least need them to. You are keenly intellectual, discriminating, and capable of dealing with details. At work, you are comfortable in a secondary position, as long as your efforts are appreciated. You are embarrassed by displays of emotion, but can lose your temper, shout, and be cutting when upset.

You are a good cook and homemaker, and you probably have a pet. Not all of you

are happy in a permanent relationship, because you maintain a detached and independent attitude. You might not like overt displays of affection, but you are kind, loving, and highly sexed.

MOON IN LIBRA

Being charming, optimistic, outgoing, and sociable, you are a skilled and tactful diplomat who is popular at work and in social settings—and the chances are you are also nice looking. You are not as soft as you appear, because you are actually ambitious and determined, especially when you have a goal in sight.

Friends, relatives, and lovers are all welcome additions to your home and your life, but those who seek to monopolize you or drain you won't be allowed to stay long. You can be very faithful in the right relationship, but this doesn't prevent you from flirting.

MOON IN SCORPIO

Your emotions are close to the surface. It is possible for you to hold down a mundane job, but hobbies or spare time interests have real meaning and will balance this.

You prefer to be in a meaningful relationship. You are unlikely to let your partner down, and you will not forgive someone who is disloyal to you. There is always some part of your life that you like to keep to yourself—perhaps a small savings account or a few photographs from your past. This is a notably sexy moon placement—and for you, sex and love are absolutely entwined.

MOON IN SAGITTARIUS

An amazing number of you work as astrologers, psychics, or ministers of religion because your moon urges you to do something meaningful. You

might work with horses or with other large animals.

Your family background might be different from the surrounding culture, so there is a need to move smoothly between cultures and to understand both. You might reject your parents' religion or view of life.

MOON IN CAPRICORN

Your childhood experiences will have shown you that life can be hard. It takes you a long time to climb the ladder of success, but your application and determination mean you will make it. You instinctively know you are likely to have a long life, so there is plenty of time for you to make up for a slow start. You take care of your parents and family.

MOON IN AQUARIUS

Your early life was hard, which leads you to push hard to make a success of yourself, but once you reach a comfortable middle age, you might become rebellious or strange. You cannot be dictated to because you prefer to do it your way, but you have the knack of getting on with all kinds of people. You have strong likes and dislikes, but like or dislike people for who they are rather than on grounds of race, religion, or culture.

MOON IN PISCES

You might choose an unusual lifestyle. Being extremely sensitive, you can tune in psychically to others and perhaps also feel the future before it arrives. Childhood experiences left a major mark on you, leaving you vulnerable, sensitive, easily hurt, and upset. This gives you an uncanny talent for understanding the underdog, which might lead you into a caring career. You can be a talented photographer, dancer or entertainer. With true love, you will blossom.

Ms. Wimp revealed

Ms. Wimp's sun, moon, and rising signs all reveal her character.

Here, we go through all of the major features that are found on

the chart. She turned out to be a very interesting young woman.

SUN IN ARIES
IN THE SEVENTH HOUSE

The sun in the quick-thinking fire sign of Aries means Ms. Wimp is a hard worker and has a strong character. Aries is the least wimpish of all the signs, but Arians can lose faith in themselves, so they need a supportive partner. While Ms. Wimp demands loyalty from a lover, she can still be tempted into a quick fling if she feels that her relationship is becoming restrictive or boring. Idealism, coupled with an interest in politics, can lead her into teaching because this combines helping others and a strong dose of political maneuvering.

Sun in the seventh house makes her likeable and fond of companionship. Despite the independence of Aries, she needs a partner who will approve of her, appreciate her, validate her, and build her self-confidence. She can also be in two minds when decision-time looms.

20° ♊ 54'

54'

♋ 54'

20°

20° ♉ 54'

MC
20° ♊ 04'

♂ 04° ♊ 27'

♄ 02° ♊ 58'

♀ 29° ♉ 03'

20°

♈ 54'

☉

☿

21' ♈ 13° 08°
48' ♈
Rx

20° ♓ 54'

Sun in Aries
in the seventh house

Rx

25' Rx

Rx
09'

♒ 02°

♌

54'

20°

Rx
00' 04°
♏ ♐
29° 05°
☽ ♆

34'
♑
07°

♃

54'

54'

20°

Moon in Scorpio in the third house

20° ♏ 54'

20° ♐ 54'

VIRGO RISING

Adds intelligence and capability, so Ms. Wimp has a well-organized and analytical mind, and a talent for writing or communicating. The Virgo connection might promote an interest in health and healing, but it can also take her into teaching and writing. Virgo rising indicates a difficult childhood with at least one highly critical parent. The Aries/Virgo mixture encouraged Ms. Wimp to leave home early, while the seventh house connection might have taken her into an early marriage.

Virgo rising undermines self-worth and makes it hard for Ms. Wimp to believe she is entitled to anything, so she shoots herself in the foot whenever success looms near. This ascendant is linked to the sign of Pisces at its opposite end (the descendant). Both signs are associated with self-sacrifice, so Ms. Wimp is drawn to weak lovers who need to be rescued. The lovers are drawn to the apparent strength of her Aries sun sign, while completely missing the fact that Ms. Wimp can appear outwardly capable, but her ego needs to be propped up.

MOON IN SCORPIO
IN THE THIRD HOUSE

Scorpio gives her sexual magnetism and a strong sex drive, and intense feelings, and she can be possessive and jealous. She experiences a great deal of inner pain. The moon in the third house suggests she has a love/hate relationship with brothers and sisters. This moon position also adds to Ms. Wimp's ability to investigate, research, communicate, write, teach, and think deeply. She lacks the ability to negotiate successfully, either at work or for her emotional requirements, so she gives way, becomes resentful, and then loses her temper.

Uranus in Libra in the first house indicates that our industrious Ms. Wimp is happy to study for a brighter future.

More of Ms. Wimp revealed

MERCURY IN ARIES
IN THE SEVENTH HOUSE

Mercury allows Ms. Wimp to present herself well to others (seventh house), but she can be opinionated (Aries). Her mind is quick, and sarcastic comments pop out of her mouth before she can stop herself.

VENUS IN TAURUS
IN THE NINTH HOUSE

Makes her charming and attractive, but it can add to her possessiveness regarding people and possessions, and it can make her self-indulgent. This is at odds with her sacrificial and idealistic side. The ninth house suggests that, despite her longing for security, there is a parallel need for freedom.

MARS AND SATURN IN GEMINI
IN THE NINTH HOUSE

She loves to explore ideas, philosophies, religions, and spiritual interests. Saturn sometimes represents the father, and hers prefers a detached relationship to a close one. The moon often represents the mother, so her moon in Scorpio might denote a heavy-handed or demanding mother. The moon being on the opposite side of the chart from Saturn suggests that her parents are at odds with each other.

NEPTUNE IN SAGITTARIUS
IN THE THIRD HOUSE

The moon close by Neptune in the freedom-loving sign of Sagittarius suggests that at least one parent (the father) escaped and abandoned Ms. Wimp to her fate. The men in her life (Mars close to Saturn) repeat this pattern. Her capacity for giving and receiving love is ruled by Venus, which is too close to hard-faced, gloomy old Saturn for comfort. The opposition between the Venus/Saturn/Mars conjunction and the moon/Neptune one makes it hard for her to draw trustworthy people around her.

PLUTO RISING IN LIBRA
IN THE FIRST HOUSE

Resentful, emotional, and powerful Pluto rises in Libra, suggesting that she tries over and again to solve her traumas (Pluto) through relationships (Libra). As Libra is a talkative air sign and Virgo rising is also very talkative, she struggles to make men listen and to understand her.

Ms. Wimp is inclined to be slightly cheeky, as well as charming and attractive. (Venus in Taurus in the ninth house.)

URANUS IN LIBRA
IN THE FIRST HOUSE

Ms. Wimp is gradually finding her way out of her emotional maze by studying subjects such as psychology and astrology. Uranus also gives her a very keen mind, intuition, and an ability to solve problems. This planet's opposition to the sun can make her very original, but it can also hamper her success by making her sarcastic, stubborn, and awkward at times.

JUPITER IN CAPRICORN
IN THE FOURTH HOUSE

Our heroine can make money if she invests in property. In time, she might open a school for esoteric subjects. Jupiter is in square aspect to the sun and businesslike Mercury, so she will need a trustworthy partner to negotiate for her. Trines to the north node of the moon confirm that property matters will be a success.. In time, she might even make peace with her mother (trine aspect to nodes).

Ms. Wimp is arguing with the planet Mars, which is in Gemini in her ninth House. Who wins?

Looking at Ms. Wimp's aspects

On various pages you saw a circle with a collection of intriguing red and blue lines in the center of Ms. Wimp's chart. These are the aspect lines. Some aspects on a chart are easy to live with, while others are difficult. The red lines in the center of a chart are difficult aspects (such as the square and the opposition); the blue lines are easy aspects (such as the sextile and trine). Let's use Ms. Wimp's chart as an example while working our way through the planetary aspects.

Aspects between planets have to be within a certain number of degrees. Astrologers don't all agree on exactly what these orbs should be, but most would be happy with the ones I suggest here.

THE CONJUNCTION

• From zero to 10 degrees apart.

This is when two or more planets are close to each other. If you look at Venus, Mars, and Saturn in the chart, you will see three planets in conjunction. The fact that Venus is in a different sign from the other two planets makes no difference. Venus is in the very last degree of Taurus (29 degrees Taurus), while Saturn is almost at 3 degrees of Gemini and Mars is at 4 degrees of Gemini.

This means that all three planets are within 10 degrees of each other, so they are in conjunction.

THE SEXTILE
• 60 degrees apart.
• Allowed orb of six degrees.

Sextiles are marked on the chart with blue lines. In Ms. Wimp's case, the moon and Neptune are both sextile to Pluto. In addition, both the moon and Neptune are sextile to the north node of the moon, which is in Aquarius; the triple conjunction of Venus/Mars/Saturn is sextile to the south node; and Pluto is also sextile to the south node.

THE SQUARE
• 90 degrees apart.
• Allowed orb of six degrees.

Squares are marked on the chart by red lines. Ms. Wimp has her sun/Mercury conjunction in square aspect to Jupiter.

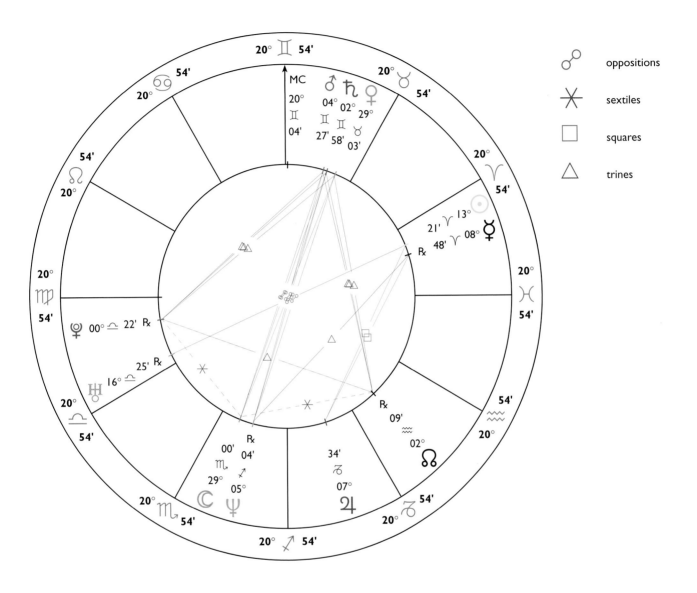

oppositions

sextiles

squares

trines

THE TRINE

- 120 degrees apart
- Allowed orb, six degrees

The trines on Ms. Wimp's chart are marked in blue. She has a trine from the Venus/Mars/Saturn conjunction to Pluto, another from this conjunction to the north node, and another from Pluto to the north node. This makes a grand trine. In addition, there is a trine from the moon/Neptune conjunction to the south node, and another from Uranus to the midheaven.

THE OPPOSITION

- Opposite each other
- 180 degrees apart
- Allowed orb of eight degrees

Oppositions are shown by red lines. Ms. Wimp has the Venus/Mars/Saturn conjunction opposite her moon/Jupiter conjunction. She also has the sun/Mercury conjunction opposite her Uranus.

Aspects of life

Challenging aspects play an important role because they force us to overcome problems, promoting psychological growth. Nice ones alleviate a difficult chart and bring fun into everyday life.

CONJUNCTION (0 DEGREES)

A conjunction can be easy or challenging, depending upon the planets involved. For example, a sun/Venus conjunction can mean a pleasing personality and luck in love, money, and possessions. However, a Venus/Saturn conjunction might bring hard times in connection with these matters, and possibly poor health into the bargain.

SEXTILE (60 DEGREES)

A sextile aspect is fortunate, especially where learning, intellect, and bright ideas are concerned. It can bring luck in career matters, friendships, and communication issues. Even difficult planets have their good sides, and they really shine in a sextile aspect.

SQUARE (90 DEGREES)

A square aspect is probably the most challenging of all the aspects, because it always means some kind of fight or perhaps endurance is needed to cope with it. This is where we learn to build on our strengths and work on our weaknesses.

TRINE (120 DEGREES)

This is a pleasant aspect that promotes creativity and brings fun and joy into our lives. Even a difficult planet has a strong and useful side to its nature, and these qualities come into their own in a trine aspect.

OPPOSITION (180 DEGREES)

This brings relationships with others to the fore. These can be enhanced by the kinder planets, but there can be obstruction and difficulties to face in any kind of contact with others if the planets are difficult.

There are other aspects, but the only one worth considering at this stage might be the conjunction, which puts two planets 150 degrees apart and can be an irritating aspect.

THE NODES OF THE MOON

These are an astronomical feature that relate to the places where the path of the moon crosses the path of the sun. On a chart, the north node brings karmic benefits and makes life easy; the south node can also have this effect, but aspects are less likely to be as effective or positive as those to the north node. Anything relating to the nodes can bring luck in family and domestic affairs, career, and other aspirations and spiritual development.

SOME GOOD ASPECTS

As you can see on Ms. Wimp's chart on the previous page, there are trines from the Venus/Saturn/Mars conjunction to Pluto, and they can help her turn her life around once she reaches a level of understanding. The third trine between Pluto and the north node completes a grand trine, which endows Ms. Wimp with talent and creativity. Venus gives her a talent for singing, dancing, and art, which may eventually bring success and the touch of fame she needs.

Here the two planets, Neptune (this page) and the Sun (opposite page), are in opposition.

Transits

The art of predicting the future lies in transits which refer to the position of the planets at any one time. Much of what you have read can now be applied to predicting the future.

The birth chart shows where everything is at the time of birth, however, if you wish to look at your situation as it is at present, and as it will unfold in the coming weeks, months, and years, you will need to investigate the transits. Every astrologer uses this technique, comparing birth chart with a chart of the date under investigation, and refers to the fact that a planet has moved into or out of your sign, or is making an aspect to your sun.

You can buy an ephemeris, a book of tables which shows where each planet is on any day in any year. With practice, you will soon be able to pencil the position of the transiting planets outside your birth chart. Then you can check how each transiting planet affects the sign and house it is moving through, and also check out the aspects that it makes to any planet on your birth chart. Ask a friend who knows how to do this method, or an astrologer, to explain what to do, and I promise you that you will get the hang of transits within five minutes.

However you find the planetary positions, from your computer program, an internet service, or an astrologer, you will end up with two sets of planets to consider. The first are those on your birth chart, and the second set is the transits as they are on the day you wish to investigate.

Take a few fine-tipped colored pens and write the glyphs for the transiting planets around the outside of your birth chart. For example, if Pluto is in Sagittarius on the date you are examining, pencil the glyph for Pluto outside the Sagittarius section of the chart.

Check out the houses that these planets occupy to see how they affect the issues that each of the houses relates to. For instance, if Mars is transiting your fourth house of home and family, chances are you will soon change your address, or make changes to your life which affect your parents and family.

Look at the aspects between each planet. See if one planet crosses another, or runs opposite it, or makes a sextile. square, or trine aspect to it. If a planet of happiness such as Venus or Jupiter makes a trine to your sun, or to something else on the chart, you can be sure you will soon have something to celebrate!

The date chosen to illustrate transits for Ms. Wimp was July 4, 2005. Let's see what lies in store for her. **The sun** is at 13 degrees Cancer in her 10th house of aims and aspirations. If she finds courage within herself she can reach out for what she wants in life. July 4 will bring a minor setback while the sun makes a square aspect to her natal sun in Aries.

The moon is at 26 degrees Gemini in her 10th house. The moon moves so quickly that it will only be in this house for a day or two, but it suggests that her women relatives, friends, and colleagues will be around to help her.

Mercury and Venus are in conjunction at 8 degrees of Leo in her 11th house of influential friends. These planets form a trine to her Mercury and they are moving toward a trine to her sun. Mercury could take her to a party or an event in her neighborhood, and romantic Venus suggests that she could meet an interesting new man.

Magnetic Mars is at 15 degrees of Aries in her seventh house of relationships, and it will soon move into her eighth house of commitment and union. Surely the next few weeks will bring Ms. Wimp the love and excitement she craves?

Jolly Jupiter is at 10 degrees of Libra in her first house of self and it will remain there for several months. She must seize the opportunities for adventure, change, and expansion of her horizons.

Serious Saturn is at 28 degrees of Cancer in her 11th house of hopes, wishes, and friendship, and it will soon make trine aspects to Venus (love) and the moon (emotions, home, and family). Saturn represents things that endure, so the romance hovering on the horizon will turn out to be rock solid.

MS. WIMP'S TRANSITS FOR JULY 4, 2005

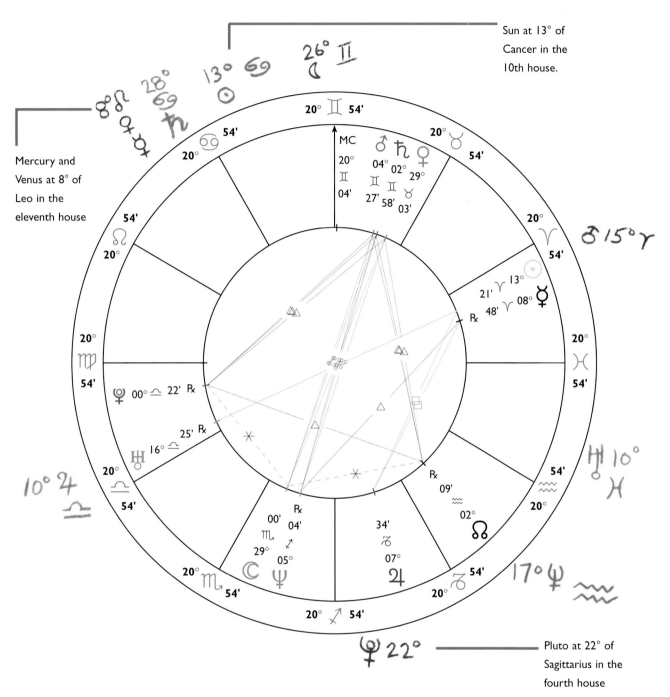

Sun at 13° of Cancer in the 10th house.

Mercury and Venus at 8° of Leo in the eleventh house

Pluto at 22° of Sagittarius in the fourth house

Unpredictable Uranus is at 10 degrees of Pisces in her sixth house of work and health. It is not making any major aspects, although it will form an inconjunct to her natal Uranus later in the year. This will bring unexpected changes at work or health problems.

Nebulous Neptune is at 17 degrees of Aquarius in her fifth house of romance. It has recently made a trine to her natal Uranus, so the chances are that love has, or is now, on the point of racing into her life.

Pluto is at 22 degrees of Sagittarius in her fourth house of home and family. Although it is not making any aspects right now, it will be in this position for several years, so the chances of improving her family life are excellent.

How strange it is that purely by chance the date I picked links with a period of time when Ms. Wimp will find her Mr Right—and the outlook appears that she will live happily ever after from this point onwards!

Everybody wants to know what she or he is like, and what is likely to happen in life—and that is what a wimp can discover through astrology. Let us take a fun break and look at some of the characteristics of each sun sign.

other things

a wimp needs to know

Signs in a nutshell

Here are a few typical features of the signs for you to learn. Try recognizing these characteristics in your friends.

ARIES

Body areas	Head, eyes, skull, and upper jaw. Often red-headed when young, and many men lose their hair in middle age. Usually has a small nose and chin, and full cheeks.
Best qualities	Energy and initiative, a capacity for hard work, and a love of life
Worst qualities	Selfishness, vanity, impatience, and aggression
Weaknesses	Fast cars, fast lovers, and buying more clothes than you need
Food weaknesses	Fast food, alcohol, and creamy dishes
Best day	Tuesday
Worst day	Friday
Color	Red
Metal	Iron
Gems	Diamond and bloodstone

TAURUS

Body areas	Lower jaw, throat, including thyroid gland, neck, and upper spine. Males hide their looks with glasses, beards, and hair; females hide their looks with layers of cosmetics.
Best qualities	Thoroughness, care with money, and patience
Worst qualities	Obstinacy and possessiveness
Weaknesses	Money and possessions
Food weaknesses	Cakes and candy
Best day	Friday
Worst day	Tuesday
Colors	Green and pink
Metal	Copper
Gems	Emerald, topaz, and sapphire

GEMINI

Body areas	The upper respiratory system, shoulders, arms, wrists, and hands; worry about putting on weight.
Best qualities	Mental agility, adaptability, and a great sense of humor
Worst qualities	Lack of sympathy when others are ill or unhappy
Weaknesses	Chatting on the phone for hours, and either smoking or making a huge fuss when others do so
Food weaknesses	None
Best day	Wednesday
Worst day	Friday
Color	Yellow
Metal	Mercury
Gems	Agate and onyx

CANCER

Body areas	Lungs, breasts, rib cage, stomach, and digestive organs.
Best qualities	Good listener, kindhearted, and sympathetic friend
Worst qualities	Moody and bad-tempered without knowing why, and you cling to your family
Weaknesses	Worry about nothing
Food weaknesses	Chocolate, cakes, and those door stopper sandwiches

Best day	Monday
Worst day	Wednesday
Colors	White and silver
Metal	Silver
Gems	Pearl and mother-of-pearl

Nutshells continued

LEO

Body parts	Spine, heart, arteries, and circulation; worry about hair—males are worse than females!
Best qualities	Honesty, generosity, and a talent for organization
Worst qualities	Arrogance, irritability, vanity, and extravagance
Weaknesses	Falls in love too quickly
Food weaknesses	None. You love to dine in expensive restaurants.
Best day	Sunday
Worst day	Saturday
Colors	Gold, yellow, cream, and orange
Metal	Gold
Gems	Diamond, zircon, and tiger's eye

VIRGO

Body parts	Digestive system, bowels, skin, nervous system, and the mind
Best qualities	Kindhearted and patient, with an eye for the detail needed for both art and craft work. A sense of the ridiculous, can make others laugh
Worst qualities	Fussy, critical, and hypochondriac. Low self-esteem, wither under criticism
Weaknesses	Buying books
Food weaknesses	Quick-to-prepare-and-eat foods
Best day	Wednesday
Worst day	Thursday
Colors	Navy blue, muted green, brown
Metal	Mercury
Gems	Lace agate and chrysolite

LIBRA

Body areas	Bladder and kidneys, and lower spine
Best qualities	Pleasant, charming, and friendly, fair minded; a good arbitrator
Worst qualities	Indecisive and unrealistic, talk more than do
Weaknesses	Luxury
Food weaknesses	Alcohol and dessert

Best day	Friday
Worst day	Wednesday
Colors	Green and pink
Metal	Copper
Gems	Sapphire, emerald, and jade

SCORPIO

Body areas	Sexual organs, lower stomach, lower spine, and groin; also blood and eyes

Best qualities	Endurance, tenacity, will power, self-control, protective toward family
Worst qualities	Can be secretive, suspicious, inflexible, vindictive, and ruthless
Weaknesses	Sex
Food weaknesses	Alcohol, sweets, and chocolates
Best day	Tuesday
Worst day	Friday
Colors	Dark red and dark purple
Metal	Iron
Gems	Opal, obsidian, onyx, and jet

Nutshells continued

SAGITTARIUS

Body areas	Hips, thighs, and circulation through the legs
Best qualities	Wonderful sense of humor, intelligence, and honesty; values are spiritual, not materialistic

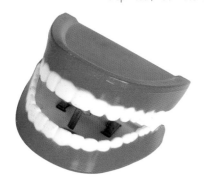

Worst qualities	Tactlessness, restlessness, and an inability to be realistic
Weaknesses	Travel
Food weaknesses	Liking only a small range of foods
Best day	Thursday
Worst day	Saturday
Colors	Royal blue and Imperial purple
Metal	Tin
Gems	Topaz, carbuncle, and sapphire

CAPRICORN

Body areas	Skin, ears, bones, knees, and teeth
Best qualities	Hard-working, family-minded; good sense of humor, realistic
Worst qualities	Can be dull and dry, stingy, and lacking in imagination
Weaknesses	Snobbishness and a fondness for status symbols
Food weaknesses	Rich menus
Best day	Saturday
Worst day	Thursday
Colors	Gray, dark green, and brown
Metal	Lead
Gems	Turquoise, black opal, and tourmaline

AQUARIUS

Body areas	Ankles, skin, lungs, and circulation
Best qualities	Friendliness, independence, and intelligence
Worst qualities	Rebelliousness, eccentricity, forgetfulness
Weaknesses	Gadgets
Food weaknesses	Salty snacks, such as potato chips, olives, and pickles

Best day	Saturday
Worst day	Monday
Colors	Electric blue and indigo
Metal	Uranium
Gems	Lapis lazuli and amethyst

PISCES

Body areas	Feet, mind, and lungs
Best qualities	Imagination, sensitivity, and artistry
Worst qualities	Indecision, inclined to worry over nothing, and lack will power
Weaknesses	Escapism
Food weaknesses	Alcohol and anything fattening
Best day	Thursday
Worst day	Wednesday
Colors	Green-blues, turquoise, and purple
Metal	Tin
Gems	Moonstone and pearl

Chart interpretation

As a beginner you have a choice of two ways to begin the process of interpretation. In time you will discover the best way for you. Some astrologers start with the rising sign and work around the chart in a counterclockwise direction, looking at each sign, house, and planet or other factor in turn. Others start with the rising sign, move on to analyze the sun, then the moon sign, followed by each planet in turn and ending with the midheaven and nodes (page 21) of the moon.

Behind this cuddly exterior lurks an intuitive and spiritual soul with a tendency to sacrifice herself for others.

Check your findings with the person you are analyzing and get feedback from them, because a birth chart, like a personality, is layered.

The ability to weigh up a chart is the difference between the activity of a good astrologer and just receiving a chart in the mail from an astrology service. The kind of background and childhood influences that the rising sign relates to are so imprinted they often dictate the way a person acts when they are unsure of themselves.

The rising sign can affect a person's outer behavior because that is how they have been programmed to behave, but in a more confident person, the sun sign or something else on the chart might shine through.

Those whose feelings are more on the surface might exhibit more of their moon sign (especially when young), while those who seek to cover up their true feelings and motives will have a moon sign tucked well away.

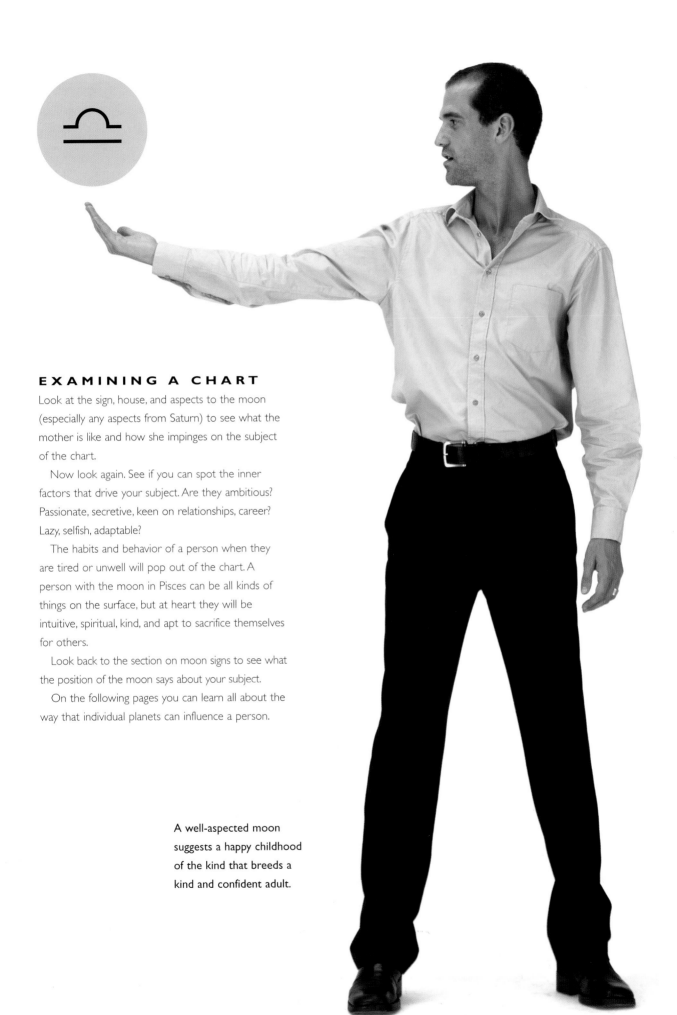

EXAMINING A CHART

Look at the sign, house, and aspects to the moon (especially any aspects from Saturn) to see what the mother is like and how she impinges on the subject of the chart.

Now look again. See if you can spot the inner factors that drive your subject. Are they ambitious? Passionate, secretive, keen on relationships, career? Lazy, selfish, adaptable?

The habits and behavior of a person when they are tired or unwell will pop out of the chart. A person with the moon in Pisces can be all kinds of things on the surface, but at heart they will be intuitive, spiritual, kind, and apt to sacrifice themselves for others.

Look back to the section on moon signs to see what the position of the moon says about your subject.

On the following pages you can learn all about the way that individual planets can influence a person.

A well-aspected moon suggests a happy childhood of the kind that breeds a kind and confident adult.

How planets work on you!

MERCURY

Mercury is similar in nature to the sign of Gemini and to the third house, and also to Virgo and the sixth house, so if you have a handle on the signs, you can see what Mercury is all about. If you then apply Mercury to the sign it is in, to see how it acts, and the house to see what it is trying to achieve, you will have the idea.

For example, Mercury rules the mentality and communication talent, so it will be far more intellectual and talkative in Gemini and Aquarius than it will in Capricorn or Pisces. However, in the fourth house, the subject's thoughts and conversation will be about family and property matters.

VENUS

Venus is similar to the signs of Taurus and Libra, and it connects with the second and seventh houses, so these signs will help you understand the planet and the houses. Venus is about the things we value and love—personal finances, personal possessions, the principles, and people we value. It also relates to our self-image and self-confidence, so if somebody or something attacks us, you can be sure Venus will show this.

Venus rules acceptable and open relationships, but it also shows those who seek to attack us. It relates to justice, fair play, and balance. For example, Venus in Libra may represent a peacemaker, an arbitrator, a relater, and an artistic person, but in the competitive first house, this person can be aggressive and argumentative. Venus in Virgo cannot be touchy-feely or demonstrative, but in the fifth house, this person shows love by doing things for their loved ones.

MARS

Gentle wimps might not want to admit to having this assertive, competitive planet anywhere near their horoscope charts, but without a Mars, you wouldn't be able to get up in the morning. Mars relates to Aries and the first house. This gives you the drive to get through the day, as well as the drive to get things done and to succeed.

Consider whether Mars is in an assertive, intellectual, peaceable, or emotional sign. For example, Mars in Scorpio is great for digging out information, which might be useful for a student of history in the fourth, a policewoman in the eighth, or a student of astrology in the eleventh.

JUPITER

Jupiter links to Sagittarius and the ninth house, all of which are interested in pushing back boundaries and exploring the unknown. Jupiter is a restless planet, so it can take a person on voyages, or even cause them to emigrate, but it also rules the philosophy and principles we live by. It is concerned with manmade and spiritual laws, thus of karma and belief. It is considered a lucky planet, associated with gambling and speculating. Jupiter also rules large animals.

Jupiter in Sagittarius in the sixth might encourage a person to work in a zoo or a game preserve. In Pisces in the seventh, it might belong to a preacher. In Taurus in the eighth, it might involve a person in a protracted legal battle over taxes, corporate matters, or an inheritance.

SATURN

Saturn relates to Capricorn and the tenth house, both concerned with goals and ambitions. Newcomers to astrology always get wimpy when it comes to Saturn. They complain that Saturn is the cause of their hardships/money worries/dreadful marriage, and so on. Once a student of astrology learns what a hard teacher Saturn can be, they heartily wish that the gloomy planet could be moved to another solar system. Without Saturn, we couldn't finish anything we start, so it is easy to see that a bit of Saturnian effort can get you anywhere.

URANUS

Uranus is the "breakout" planet associated with Aquarius and the eleventh house, thus to revolution, original ideas, unexpected actions and events, and to turning things upside down. However, it also rules ideals and whatever is best for the group as a whole, so it can impose a kibbutz or communist mentality, seeking to keep everyone and everything on the same level. This in turn becomes restrictive, so a Uranian person will come along and break the mold.

NEPTUNE

Neptune is difficult to define. Its only relationship to the Roman god is its association with the sea and with sea voyages, so Morpheus, the god of sleep, might be a better name. Neptune rules dreams, illusions, and self-undoing, but it is also associated with artistry, music, and everything connected to psychism. It is associated with Pisces and the twelfth house.

Neptune in any sign or house that is connected to the idea of partnerships makes it hard for a person to see others clearly, so love and business relationships can go wrong. However, Neptune in the fifth house signifies artistic enterprises and beloved children—if it is also in a fire sign, the person will pursue these interests as vigorously as sleepy Neptune will allow.

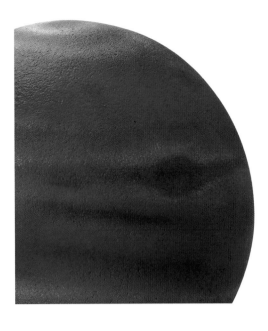

PLUTO

Pluto rules things that cannot easily be seen. In practical terms, this could be things below ground such as oil, gold, diamonds, and so on, but in psychological terms it means those undetected things that come out later and cause a major storm.

An ailment that is building up, a partner who is fooling around, or unforeseen business problems will eventually emerge and cause a major upheaval. Thus Pluto is associated with major life changes and transformation.

Pluto is associated with Scorpio and the eighth house. The planet also rules joint matters such as love or business partnerships, money that is not entirely under one's own control, and any other shared experience such as mortgages, sex, and having children.

Synastry

Synastry: now here's a word to strike fear into the heart of any pink-blooded wimp! The word, from the Greek prefix *syn*, meaning bringing together, and *astron*, meaning star, puts us in the realms of compatibility between two people. There are relationships of many different kinds in our lives, and only a few are likely to be romantic or sexual.

Taking note of your partner's good and bad qualities when deciding whether to marry can be a good thing if done in an unemotional manner.

This subject is as complicated as it is fascinating. There are many ways of approaching this synastry, and different astrologers use their own favorite methods.

However, here are a few classic ideas to try:

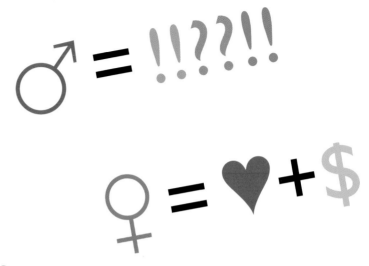

1

Examine each planet on your partner's birth chart in turn to see what aspects it makes to the planets on your chart; then assess the nature of the planets and the aspects to see which are likely to be important.

2

Assess whether there are any soft aspects such as the sextile and trine, or hard aspects such as the conjunction, square, and opposition.
The softies are likely to show the kind of easy compatibility you enjoy in a friendship.
The hard aspects bring attraction, passion, strong feelings, sexual tension, and the adjustments that have to be made in a real relationship.

These planets might supply characteristics you do not have, and which you look for in others to fill the gaps in your own personality. Indeed, the most important relationships in your life will often show squares and oppositions between the two charts. Mars will bring zest and competitiveness; Saturn will act like a wet blanket, but it will bring reliability; Venus will bring love, but also expenditure; Uranus will bring friendship, but also a touch of the unexpected.

3

Work out which house on your birth chart your partner's planets fall into, since that will have an effect on your life. If his/her planets are in your second or eighth house, money might be an issue, but if they fall into your fifth house, children and childishness might be part of the picture. Assess the sign in your seventh house to see what you want in a partner.

4

Once you have made up a full birth chart, consider your midheaven, because many successful relationships occur when one person's midheaven is the other person's sun sign, or sometimes their moon sign.

If you want to take this branch of astrology farther, look for books covering the subject in more academic detail, and study the charts of people you know to see how things work out against what you know of the dynamics of the relationship. Good luck!

Compatibility chart

Nonastrologers always ask me whether they will get along with
another of the sun-sign types. There are so many factors involved for
me to give them a quick answer! However, here is a simple, fun chart for
the basic prospects of love and compatibility between all the sun signs.

LOVE AND COMPATIBILITY CHART

	GREAT !!	GOOD	FAIR	AVOID !!
Aries	Gemini	Aquarius	Pisces	Virgo
Taurus	Taurus	Libra	Capricorn	Sagittarius
Gemini	Aries	Virgo	Aquarius	Scorpio
Cancer	Capricorn	Taurus	Pisces	Sagittarius
Leo	Libra	Scorpio	Virgo	Aries
Virgo	Cancer	Gemini	Pisces	Aries
Libra	Gemini	Leo	Aquarius	Pisces
Scorpio	Leo	Cancer	Taurus	Virgo
Sagittarius	Virgo	Capricorn	Pisces	Taurus
Capricorn	Scorpio	Cancer	Taurus	Leo
Aquarius	Aquarius	Sagittarius	Pisces	Cancer
Pisces	Pisces	Sagittarius	Aquarius	Libra

The chart on the opposite page is different from the type you see in magazines, because those are usually based on the elements. The theory being that two people with the sun in the same element will get on, but they might find it difficult to get on with some of the other elements.

Somehow, this doesn't really work in reality, so I created the compatibility chart (on the opposite page) based on many years' experience with the sun connections that *do* work.

The elements can also come into play when one person's sun sign shares the same element as another person's moon or rising sign, so if one person has the sun in the earth sign of Capricorn and the other has the moon in the earth sign of Virgo, they probably get on very well.

Here is an example of what can happen
Actress Catherine Zeta-Jones has the sun in Libra, moon in Pisces, and Sagittarius rising. Michael Douglas has his sun in Libra, moon in Capricorn, and Scorpio rising. The main link here is their Libran suns, although Catherine's emotional and watery moon makes a link with Michael's watery Scorpio ascendant.

Incidentally, papa Kirk Douglas's Sagittarian sun makes a nice match with Catherine's Sagittarian rising sign, so she probably gets on well with him, too.

Compatibility at work

Here we are not, as a rule, considering sexual attraction, but whether we can get along with people of both sexes and all ages as colleagues, employers, and employees.

If you can discover your colleague's time, date, and place of birth, you can produce a complete chart, but even if all you have to go on is a birthday, you can find the planetary positions, although you won't know the rising sign, midheaven, or the houses.

Use the basic rules of astrology. The soft aspects (sextile and trine) will be pleasant, while conjunctions could go either way. Squares are likely to be difficult; the opposition can be stressful, or it can represent a cooperative relationship where each worker values skills, talents, and characteristics the other lacks.

When considering the perfect person with whom to work, it is a good idea to look at the planet Mercury on both charts. This shows compatibility in the way two people think. An example of this might be of a Capricorn person, whose Mercury is in the adjacent sign of Aquarius, working with a Piscean whose Mercury is also in Aquarius.

If two Mercurys are in the same element this can also help. People tackle things in the same way when Mars shares the same sign or element, but these planets can complement each other and fill in each other's gaps when they are not in the same element. For example, a person with a Mars in a fire sign will make a tough negotiator or a good salesperson, while Mars in an earth sign can cope with administrative work and all that filing that's piled up!

SUN CONTACTS
provide compatibility and success, or tension and failure

MOON CONTACTS
make for a comfortable relationship, or an abrasive one

MERCURY CONTACTS
denote easy communication, or deliberate misunderstanding

VENUS CONTACTS
show shared values and similar desires, or opposing ones

MARS CONTACTS
bring assistance in difficult circumstances, or competitiveness

JUPITER CONTACTS
symbolize similarity of beliefs, or differences —and fun, or otherwise

SATURN CONTACTS
represent help from authority, or restriction and blockages

URANUS CONTACTS
bring friendship and a touch of originality —or harsh opposition

NEPTUNE CONTACTS
cause inspiration and kindness, or muddles, hidden agendas, and swindles

PLUTO CONTACTS
bring powerful influences that help you greatly, or stand in your way

These office coworkers have soft aspects that make it easy for them to work together in any situation.

Astro-handling people

Until you can get the full low-down on a person's chart, the sun sign is all you have to go on. But there are quick-and-easy ways to tap into this information to deal successfully with people you come across in everyday life. This kind of thing is downright dirty and manipulative, but for the average wimp it is a wonderful way of avoiding some of the difficulties you can encounter.

Value an Aquarian's intelligence. Stand and smile as you listen to his eloquent and inspiring words.

ARIES

Value their intelligence, knowledge, and sense of humor. If you think they lack common sense, lack interest in others, or cannot see their feelings or motives, keep this under your hat.

TAURUS

Don't ask them to lend you money, and never rush them. Value their competence, sociability, and reliability. Don't accuse the Bull of lacking intellect, and never try to make them do more than they want to do.

GEMINI

Let them tell you how hard life is, and never tell them others have a tougher time. Make much of a Gemini's knowledge and capability, but don't expect them to plow through a long and boring job. Don't criticize their spending habits.

CANCER

Talk over your problems, listen to a Cancer's problems, and give them emotional support. Value a Crab's family, even if it is awful. Don't ask a Cancer for money. Expect them to live in the past to some extent and to be moody.

LEO

Be absolutely loyal, because once you break their trust, you will never get it back. Give admiration if you genuinely feel it, but don't try to flatter a Leo as they will see straight through this strategy.

VIRGO

Value a Virgo's steadfast friendship and sense of humor. Tell them how much you value their intelligence and capacity for hard work. Don't expect them to be a successful business person. Give them personal time and space.

LIBRA

Invite a Libran to your parties and tell the person how their intelligent conversation, sense of fun, and flirtatiousness enliven these occasions. Don't ask a Libran to shoulder your problems. Be prepared for arguments—most of which will defy logic.

SCORPIO

Allow a Scorpian to think they are powerful, sexy, and important, and don't let them see that you can spot their insecurity or shortcomings. Value the love and friendship they offer, but do not allow a Scorpio to victimize you.

SAGITTARIUS

Call a Sagittarian in to fix things in your house and value them as good companions. Expect to support a Sagittarian emotionally, but don't ever cramp their style. If they have crazy opinions, don't bother to argue.

CAPRICORN

Value a Capricorn's business knowledge and reliability in the workplace; also their amazingly supportive attitude to those who they love. Don't allow the fussiness to irritate you, or the stinginess or self-centeredness to bug you.

AQUARIUS

Expect the unexpected. Value an Aquarian's intelligence and originality. Don't berate them for being forgetful, late for everything, unrealistic, or lack of sense. If they talk at you, listen quietly and try to stay awake.

PISCES

Invite this Pisces to your parties; enjoy the conviviality and their ability to sympathize with your difficulties. Accept their nutty family. Expect strange moods and that a Pisces may let you down or hurt you.

Aptitudes and careers

Here are a few sun-sign clues to talents and aptitudes, career possibilities, creativity, and

political tendencies. The sun sign is only part of the picture. The rising sign, the first

planet up after the rising sign, the midheaven, and much more relate to career choices and

aptitudes, but the sun-sign clues are useful tools.

Are you creative, intellectual, practical, or sympathetic? Your nature dictates your career choice. It's all there in your birth chart!

ARIES

Great in a large organization, a natural politician and teacher. Good with young people. Community jobs such as police and military can appeal.

TAURUS

Sensible in business—especially anything related to finance. Good at construction, creating beauty, working with the hands, singing, and entertaining.

GEMINI

Needs a job that involves communicating, getting around, and offers plenty of variety. Anything from telephone clerk, journalist, taxi driver, psychiatrist, or travel agent can appeal.

CANCER

Good with small businesses, retail, dealing with the public, real estate, looking after children, or any other kind of work-from-home small business. Some under this sign are drawn to catering.

LEO

The only position that will suffice is that of boss, so whatever field the Leo goes into, they must run their own branch, be the chairperson, or own the thing. They enjoy a glamorous job, but what a Leo really likes is a position that pays well.

VIRGO

This person accumulates knowledge, investigates ideas, and becomes an expert. Virgos don't feel comfortable taking on heavy responsibility, so the role of an expert, an administrator, or a role with attention to details will do nicely.

LIBRA

This person likes company and enjoys helping others and being appreciated. A Libran can be surprisingly lucky in business. Agency work, arbitration, and legal work might appeal, or any field that creates glamour and beauty.

SCORPIO

Despite their apparent strength, stress gets to this person, so a Scorpian prefers someone else to take ultimate responsibility or to be on show. They can be an excellent number two, a great specialist, or a wonderful salesman.

SAGITTARIUS

A host of careers appeal to this sign, but freedom and getting around is important, as is variety, so self-employment in something that interests them is a likelihood. Others do well in teaching, travel, or legal work.

CAPRICORN

If this person is not too dictatorial or unfeeling, they can run a large organization. Great with details and will work hard for whoever employs them, a Capricorn might prefer to work for or with family members.

AQUARIUS

Something oddball will appeal, but it must include variety and allow the Aquarian to do their own thing. Many Aquarians are also drawn to a career in teaching.

PISCES

This person is drawn to work in the caring professions, health, and psychic careers. Many Pisces men gravitate to bartending jobs.

Smart money

Who can handle money? Who makes it, spends it, or gives it away? The information in this section will help you to decide before you become involved with anyone!

The fire signs of Aries, Leo, and Sagittarius are good earners, but they feel that money is made to spend. Leo is likely to lavish it on their family, Aries on himself, and Sagittarius just lavishes it.

The earth signs of Taurus, Virgo, and Capricorn are all conscious that money is made flat to pile up. They might not have much, but they conserve what they have in an extremely sensible manner. Nobody can fathom the depths of their various savings accounts.

The air signs of Gemini, Libra, and Aquarius all manage to get by, but no one knows how they do it. They can fritter money away on unnecessary things, but they never really go broke.

The water signs of Cancer, Scorpio, and Pisces are all careful with money, often stingy over small things, but then spend inexplicably large sums on something they decide they want. They might have very little at times but luck (or other people) seems to rescue them just in time.

YOU LIVE WITH ??

Take note of who you live with or depend upon for money.

- If they belong to the Aries, Libra, Sagittarius, Aquarius, or Pisces signs, make sure you have something of your own to fall back on because they spend freely, or have periods of time when they do not have any work.
- You can depend on Taurus, Scorpio, and Capricorn to have funds—but don't expect them to dip into them on your behalf!
- Gemini, Cancer, Leo, Virgo, and Pisces will always support their families, even to their own detriment.
- Leo and Pisces can be real suckers when a total stranger comes to them with a good sob story.

ARIES

This person works hard, has savings, and lives well. Spends on clothes, travel, and vehicles.

TAURUS

Buys a good home, works hard, invests, and saves. Spends money on the garden, children, food, and pets (especially large, hungry dogs). Sometimes also on travel.

GEMINI

Will work at a main job and also two or three others. Spends on gadgets and clothes. A female Gemini has a shoe and handbag collection to rival that of Imelda Marcos.

CANCER

Works hard and can be seen as penny-pinching, but unexpected losses and time off eat up a Cancer's savings.

LEO

Leos can be extremely successful, but family members take advantage of their generosity, so they must institute savings plans that deduct money at source if they are not to end up in the gutter.

VIRGO

This person is a moderate earner and a good saver, so is never really without funds when times are hard.

LIBRA

Librans can go through all kinds of strange financial experiences, from huge gains to massive losses. Their best bet is to invest in a good home.

SCORPIO

When someone approaches a Scorpio with a sure-fire investment plan, they should tell them to get lost. Scorpios are neither lucky nor cool-headed when it comes to speculation.

SAGITTARIUS

A lucky gambler, so lottery tickets tend to come up. Otherwise income tends to fluctuate, so they must have something tucked away for a rainy day.

CAPRICORN

A Capricorn without a savings plan is a contradiction in terms. Whatever this person has, they will always feel that poverty is just around the corner.

AQUARIUS

It is essential for this person to be with someone who has a bit of sense, because where money is concerned, they have none at all.

PISCES

The small economies that this person practices often lead to a better standard of living later in life than others might think possible. Inheritance is also likely. The family, drink, and sheer silliness can drain money out of the coffers faster than it comes in.

Health zones

The signs of the zodiac rule various parts of the body. Read the lists here and see which parts of your body you need to look after!

ARIES / MARS
Head, eyes, face, lips, upper teeth, and hair

GEMINI / MERCURY
Shoulders, arms, wrists, hands, bronchial system, nerves, brain, pupils, and tongue

TAURUS / VENUS
Cheeks, neck, throat, lower teeth, vocal chords, and nose

LEO / THE SUN
Spine, heart, solar plexus, and pregnancy

CANCER / THE MOON
Breasts, chest, and digestive system

LIBRA / VENUS
Lower back, haunches, bladder, kidneys, and pancreas

VIRGO / MERCURY
Abdomen, intestines, nerves, and skin

SAGITTARIUS / JUPITER
Hips, thighs, sciatic nerve, and liver

SCORPIO / PLUTO
Reproductive organs and sexual organs, stomach, and lower back

CAPRICORN / SATURN
Knees, bones, joints, teeth, breathing, body hair, and skin conditions

AQUARIUS / URANUS
Calves, ankles, blood pressure, breathing, and circulation

PISCES / NEPTUNE
Feet, toes, instep, mental state, and lymph glands

How healthy are you?

There are factors other than the sun-sign relationship to parts of the body to take into account. The rising sign, moon sign, Mercury, and the sign on the cusp of the sixth house (along with any planets in the first and sixth houses) can all play a part. The main thing is not to become paranoid about health, but to remember the signs that your sun, moon, ascendant, first and sixth houses occupy, and keep an eye on any health issues that relate to them.

Some odd things can come up on a chart. For example, people with Gemini or Virgo rising often have buck teeth, while people with Mars in the first house often have red hair and scars or moles on their foreheads. There is a theory that things fall onto the heads of people who have Mars in Aries, and I once checked this out with a person who had this planetary placement. She put my finger on her head to show me that she had a dent there dating back to a time when a large cupboard had fallen on her head!

Bending over to pick up anything from the floor can cause a back injury. Always bend your knees! And Scorpios are prone to backache so they need to take extra care.

ARIES

A lack of forethought can lead to silly accidents. Aries children often fall onto their foreheads and the scars they carry testifies to their impetuosity throughout their lives. Keep a well-stocked first-aid box around to deal with minor cuts, scrapes, and scalds.

Eyes require attention, and acne and headaches can both be a problem. Arians' greatest indulgences are food and alcohol, and the best outlets for your nerves and physical condition are team games and competitive sports.

TAURUS

Keep a stock of honey, lemon juice, and some throat lozenges handy because you will suffer from sore throats. A set of strange symptoms could be caused by an under- or over-active thyroid gland. Your mouth is vulnerable, and accidents that affect your upper spine or neck can occur.

You can overindulge with cakes, candies, and cookies so weight can be a problem. To relieve tension, take up gardening and do-it-yourself work, or take your lover out dancing and walking.

GEMINI

Your delicate bronchial tubes need as much clear air as you can get into them, so a clean atmosphere, a nonsmoking regime, and walks away from city pollution will do you good. Colds tend to go to your chest. Hands, wrists, arms, and shoulders are vulnerable, and many Gemini children may break an arm. They heal well , but difficult fractures can cause problems late in life.

As a fussy eater, you can miss out on certain vitamins and minerals. Treat yourself to a twice-weekly outing, because visiting nice places and enjoying pleasant walks are good for your nerves, mind, and body. Light sports such as badminton, bowling, pool, or snooker might appeal to people in this sign.

CANCER

Coughs and colds can turn into bronchitis, so use rest, warmth, and cold remedies as soon as you become ill. Your stomach is sensitive. It is difficult to pour out your troubles to others, and sometimes your troubles take an inward journey, right to your sensitive stomach. Stress can also trigger arthritis, but despite the name of your sign, you are no more prone to cancer than any other zodiac sign.

Swimming, horse riding, and walking are all good exercise for your sign, as is something amusing like line dancing.

There's nothing worse than a swollen ankle when you want to go snowboarding! If it is seriously injured, go to the doctor. If not, rest with it on the sofa or pillow.

LEO

If your back hurts when lifting or doing anything acrobatic or strenuous, don't ignore it. Avoid heavy or rough sports, and always warm up before you start any exercise routine.

Heart trouble is not confined to Leos, but with your "A" type personality, high-blood pressure and cholesterol problems are a possibility. Long-term self-help means avoiding cigarettes and fatty foods and getting enough exercise.

Any exercise that is fun appeals to you, so try swimming, skating, skiing, dancing, or playing in the park with the children.

VIRGO

You can suffer from constipation and other problems, such as irritable bowel syndrome. Make sure your kitchen and bathroom are scrupulously clean, and wash all raw foodstuffs. Buy organic foods, especially fresh fruit, breakfast cereal, and other regulating foodstuffs. Skin problems such as eczema or psoriasis can bother you until you learn how to deal with them.

You are not particularly self-indulgent where food is concerned, but you might snack rather than make proper meals.

Aromatherapy, massage, or anything that soothes the nerves is good for you, as is gentle exercise such as yoga, gardening, and, best of all, having a laugh with your friends.

LIBRA

The Libran weak spots are bladder and kidneys, so drink plenty of water and cranberry juice and avoid strong coffee or alcohol. Kidney problems are uncommon, but if they occur they always require urgent medical attention. Your self-indulgence where food and alcohol are concerned can lead to diabetes and heart disease.

You are probably an excellent dancer, and golf, fishing, pool, snooker, tennis, and other slow but competitive sports might appeal.

SCORPIO

Exercise throughout your life will help keep the delicate muscles and bones of your lower back in good condition. Your stomach might also be sensitive, especially under stress. If you are a typical Scorpio, you can forget to eat if you are busy, so take a homemade lunch to work. The reproductive organs can trouble Scorpios, so don't ignore problems.

You can cope with and enjoy any kind of team game or competitive sports, and you could be a good dancer, swimmer, mud-wrestler, or skier. Do some kind of exercise at least three times a week to keep yourself sane and your family from throwing you out.

SAGITTARIUS

Later in life, rheumatism might set into your hips, so stay active throughout your life, take calcium supplements, and avoid the acid foods that seem to aggravate rheumatism. Your other weak spot is your liver, so protect yourself against hepatitis and drink plenty of water and eat fresh, green foods.

If your diet is restricted by dislike of certain foods, take vitamins to balance it. Some Sagittarians get enough exercise at work and only need the odd walk or ball game with the kids as a top-up.

Others love all kinds of sports, including riding horses, winter sports, and something crazy like hang-gliding or bungee-jumping.

CAPRICORN

Your biggest problem is your hearing, and weak knees, shins, and calves can make life difficult. Capricorn rules the skeleton, so make sure you get enough calcium to help keep your bones strong. You are not sporty, but you enjoy gentle activities like gardening and dancing, which will help keep you mobile.

You might not be particularly fussy about what you eat but problems can arise from your busy lifestyle. Restaurants offer a wide variety of excellent fresh foods, so if you have frequent business lunches, choose your menus for their nutrition content rather than for either economy or status. If you can't get out to eat, take a packed lunch to work. Dancing, singing, or light sporting activities should appeal.

AQUARIUS

Your traditional weak spots are your ankles, but your whole skeleton might not be strong and you can suffer from back problems. Some Aquarians are asthmatic, and others have hayfever or eczema. An herbal specialist might be able to treat any skin problems. Many of you have poor circulation, or might suffer from varicose veins or phlebitis. Mouth ulcers are associated with your sign, but can be avoided by taking vitamin A and D supplements.

Keep active in any way you enjoy. Slightly unusual sports might interest you, or you may be adventurous enough to try anything as long as it doesn't hurt your ankles. Try yoga, tai-chi, karate, or judo.

PISCES

Your traditional weak spot is your feet. If you overdo alcohol, your sensitive liver will object. You might gain weight later in life, so go out dancing as often as you can. Pisceans are excellent dancers, and rhythmical music feeds something in your soul. Some of you love swimming, tai-chi, or yoga.

INDEX

THE SUN-SIGN STARS

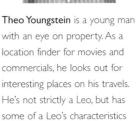

Emma McKelvie, Arian and Ms. Wimp, enjoys traveling and working in creative areas. As a journalist and stylist, her work takes her to many countries, adding to her wealth of experience.

Pamela Lin works for an investment company and enjoys most of the things associated with the sun sign of Taurus. She was not too surprised by the findings worked out by Sasha.

Theo Youngstein is a young man with an eye on property. As a location finder for movies and commercials, he looks out for interesting places on his travels. He's not strictly a Leo, but has some of a Leo's characteristics

Yumi is a typical Gemini and loves to talk on the telephone! An international soul, Yumi has a small child to amuse during the day, which is great because she has a wonderful sense of humor!

Agnes LeNart is a true New Yorker, turning up at the shoot wearing Manolo Blahniks! We loved her and her predictions for the planet Neptune. During the day she works in the fashion department of *Vanity Fair* magazine.

Sarah Cartwright is an actress and is interested in all aspects of astrology. To keep busy she also takes part in role-playing situations for business organizations and finds it teaches her a great deal about people and their behavior.

Clair Wayman is one of the luckiest people born under the sign of Virgo. She has moved to Melbourne, Australia, and the stars look good for her future.

Peter Broome, an actor, was our Aquarian, and was up for anything! The most amusing memory from the shoot involved Sasha holding his feet while he stood on his head, and someone else held the planet between his legs. That's all we're saying about that day.

astrology for wimps

Juliette Malley is a Capricorn in all of the best ways, and a great dancer! Her energetic and friendly contribution to a shoot held on a cold and rainy day in late summer was very welcome.

Craig Madgewick works as an event organizer, so nothing surprises him! This appearance was a last-minute decision and in keeping with his sun-sign character! We had to keep him from getting carried away with the power drill!

ACKNOWLEDGMENTS

To the millions of people who have bought my books, the thousands of people for whom I have given readings, and the hundreds I have taught, thanks! Everything I have done has taught me something about astrology—and about life.

The BookMaker would like to thank Badcock & Fruitful for creating the planets for the photographs, and the 12 sun sign stars for being willing to appear with nothing more than a planet and their imagination. Thanks to Mary for being down to earth, and to James and Amanda for their approach to Wimps!

Jane Bolsover is a media star and a true Sagittarian always ready to travel anywhere! Quick to have a laugh and be the star of any night out, Jane was anything but a wimp on this shoot.

Clair Smith, our valiant Scorpio, was typical of that sign! Ambitious to be a successful photographer, Clair was keen to explore the digital equipment used to shoot the images in this book.

RESOURCES

If this book has stimulated your appetite sufficiently to show that you, too, can do astrology, you should consider some of the following:

Check out
www.sashafenton.com
Click through from that site to Zambezi Publishing for information on Sasha's other books. You can contact the author directly by email through this site.

Join a local astrology group and listen to the speakers who visit, or start an astrology group of your own.

Buy an astrology magazine and send off for information on astrology-by-mail courses, or practical courses held in your area.

The Urania Trust Guide to Worldwide Astrology, published by the Urania Trust, gives information on schools, organizations, software, publications, and everything else related to astrology throughout the world. UK readers can find this book and more at:

The Midheaven Bookshop
396 Caledonian Road
London N1 1DN

The Astrology Shop,
78 Neal Street,
Covent Garden,
London WC2H 9AA

For information about astrology courses and much else:
American Federation of
  Astrologers
PO Box 22040
Tempe, AZ 85285-2040

Astrologers:
Association for Astrological
  Networking (AFAN)
8306 Wilshire Boulevard
Suite 537
Beverly Hills, CA 90211

Residential courses to degree level:
Kepler College of Astrological
  Arts and Sciences
4518 University Way NE
Suite 213
Seattle, WA 98105

Charts and information:
Jeff Jawyer Astrological Services
1953 Mt. Vernon Place
Dunwoody, GA 30338

Info pack about the astrological community:
Astrology Hot Line
  Heart Centre
315 Marion Avenue
Big Rapids, MI 49307

Chart calculation services:
Astro Communication Services
PW Box 34487
San Diego, CA 92163-4487

Astro-Numeric Service
PO Box 336
Ashland, OR 97520

Microcycles
PO Box 3175
Culver City, VA 90231-3175

Computing:
Astrolabe
Box 1750
Brewster, MA 02631

Halloran Software
PO Box 75513
Los Angeles, CA 90005

Matrix Software
315 Marion Avenue
Big Rapids, MI 49037

For pocket computers:
Astrologic
Varnum Associates Inc
Route 3,
Box 182
Luray, VA 22835

Buy some software and make up as many charts for as many people as you can find. For you are no longer an astrological wimp if you've reached this far!